Rupert Morris is a w
has spent twenty ye
newspapers and ma
years as a staff reporter on the *Daily Telegraph*
and five years on *The Times*. In 1991 he wrote
Tories, a book about grass-roots politics. He
now runs his own company, writing speeches
and running courses and workshops in
effective writing skills for businesses and
public bodies. He is assistant editor of *The
Week*, a weekly review of the best of the
British and international print media.

The
RIGHT
WAY
to
WRITE

How to write
effective
business letters,
reports, memos
and e-mail

RUPERT MORRIS

PIATKUS

Dedication

In memory of my father, Malcolm Morris, and with thanks to Ivor Abelson, whose letter-writing abilities will be appreciated for a long while yet.

Copyright © 1998 by Rupert Morris

First published in 1998 by
Judy Piatkus (Publishers) Ltd of
5 Windmill Street, London W1P 1HF

This paperback edition published in 1999

The moral right of the author has been asserted

*A catalogue record for this book is
available from the British Library*

ISBN 0–7499–1838–1 (hbk)
     0–7499–1878–0 (pbk)

Designed by Paul Saunders
Typeset by Action Typesetting Limited, Gloucester
Printed and bound in Great Britain by
Biddles Ltd, Guildford & King's Lynn

Contents

Acknowledgements

My sister Laura was the best agent I could have had. Rachel Winning has been a constructive and inspiring editor. I am grateful to Graham Jones, who spotted the roadsign mentioned in Chapter 2, and to all my former colleagues at The Company Writers for their ideas and moral support. Finally, my thanks to everyone at Clarity, particularly Sally Byrne for her dependability and cheerfulness, and Victoria Nicolaou, whose thoughtful suggestions added crucial elements to the text.

Introduction: How to Use this Book

Too many people write correspondence with the aim of sounding important, or of putting up a defence – not to communicate. This book can help you break free from negative habits and learn to write with purpose – so that you get the results you want. And if you thought you couldn't write, think again.

Writing correspondence, or reports, is not some mystical art. It is simply a formalised expression of your thoughts. That means the first essential is to think clearly. You are not a machine, so stop behaving like one. You need never again start a letter with the officious expression 'Further to …' You need never end one with the tediously familiar '… please do not hesitate to contact me'. If you are reading this book, you are clearly prepared to take your writing seriously, and that's a great start.

Whether you dictate your letters, or write everything yourself; whether you are sending a short e-mail message or writing a 16-page report; you still need to start at the same place: who are you writing for, and why? Because thinking straight and 'knowing your audience' is the most important thing, this is where we start – with *The Right Approach*.

In Part II, *The Right Content*, we will consider what you want to say, and how you might say it, keeping your purpose and your reader constantly in mind. You will learn how to put together effective letters, memos, reports, e-mails and faxes for a variety of different situations. Each of these chapters contains exercises, so that you can intersperse your reading with some writing of your own. Unless the scenario is completely outside your field or experience, please try some of these exercises. In learning how to write well, there is no substitute for practical experience.

But having *The Right Content* does not mean the job is done. The French philosopher Blaise Pascal once wrote to a friend, ending with an apology: 'I'm sorry this is such a long letter,' he said. 'I didn't have time to write a short one.' Professional writers know exactly what he meant. It is one thing to get some ideas down on paper – many of us can do that and make ourselves more or less understood. But if we can polish a piece of writing so that the reader is given the essential message in as powerful and effective a form as possible, then we can really take pride in a job well done. That's why every paragraph of this book has been read – and often amended – several times, if not by me, then by my editor. And that's why Part III of this book – *The Right Style* – is just as important as the two previous parts.

The model letters, reports, e-mail messages, faxes and memos suggested in Part IV have passed through all the first three stages. They therefore provide examples of how you might achieve *The Right Result* by applying the methods explained in this book.

To get the best out of this book, you should have easy access to a reputable dictionary and relevant source material such as appropriate professional directories or *Whitaker's Almanack* (an excellent general reference book).

PART I

The Right
Approach

1. *Why Are You Writing?*

ALL SORTS of things are best dealt with in person, or on the telephone. So before you write a word, ask yourself these questions:

Should I be writing this, and if so why?
What am I trying to achieve?

Writing for yourself

Writing can be a great way of clarifying things in your own mind. If you are absolutely furious about something, and there's no one to complain to, by all means write it down. But for heaven's sake, don't send it to anyone – yet. When you read it through after the heat of the moment has subsided, you may feel quite differently. You will at least have got rid of most of your anger and given some shape to your thoughts. On reflection, you may decide you have legitimate grounds for complaint; or you may decide it's not such a big deal after all – and that it would make you look very silly if you fired off an emotional letter. Either way, you've done yourself a favour by writing it down first, while it was fresh in your mind.

It's the same with ideas, or plans. Most of us make shopping lists, don't we? So why not write other things down before you forget them? You may need to work out the implications of various business options. Or you may need to examine crucial issues involving your job, your family, your relationship, or whatever. But always be clear *why* you are writing.

And remember that at this stage, you are writing for yourself – or at least for yourself and those closest to you.

Writing for others

Writing for others – which is what this book is really about – is much more complicated. As soon as you begin to communicate with someone else, other vital considerations come into play.

'Get it in writing' is still useful advice. If, for instance, a job offer is at stake, whether you are a prospective employer or prospective employee, you don't want to get carried away in conversation, only to find on reflection that the job isn't really feasible, that there's no budget for it, or that it's a different kind of job from that originally envisaged. It can be helpful to write down what you want from the deal, and see if your opposite number can deliver it. Then you don't have to rush into anything you might regret, you have an opportunity to think it through, and there's a much better chance that you will end up with what you really want.

The only problem with the need to see things in writing is that it tends to generate information overload – usually a pile of unnecessary paperwork. So if it's not likely to achieve results, don't write it.

Before you commit yourself to writing something, you might consider the following advantages and disadvantages:

Advantages:	Disadvantages:
▪ Commitment – if it's written down, you have to act on it.	▪ Tangible evidence – which might be used against you!
▪ Time to reflect – a chance to consider something objectively.	▪ Loss of fire – losing the impetus of enthusiasm, so that the moment might be lost forever.

- Time to polish – the opportunity to ensure that your message gives exactly the right impression.

- The coldness, or distance, of print – which can imply that you don't trust your personal skills.

In deciding whether to put something in writing or not, there are only two issues that really matter – what you are trying to achieve, and what your reader is going to think. We'll come on to that in the next chapter. First, let's consider what you are trying to achieve.

What am I trying to achieve?

If you have a bright idea, by all means write it down. And if you want to share it with your colleagues, there is no handier medium than electronic mail, which can send your idea immediately to anyone who might be interested. Or you can put it in a memo and post it on the office noticeboard, or circulate it.

What you write should always depend on what you want. So the sooner you make that clear to the reader, the better. Get to the point.

Here's an internal memo from one of our leading supermarket chains:

> **Revolving Doors.** *In superstores where these doors exist, there is always comment. Even where we have an additional access door, the subject is raised. Customers would like us to remove the revolving doors.*

In the first two sentences, the reader is struggling to find out what is really going on. Where does this 'comment' come from? And is it favourable or unfavourable? 'The subject is raised' – what subject? by whom? Only in the last sentence has the writer got to the point. Suddenly everything is clear. But the two waffly sentences in front fatally reduce the urgency of the message.

Here's another internal memo:

> *Owing to the need to reduce costs and introduce economies into the significant spend which is currently incurred in the shipping of our products, it has been decided to merge the two shipping administrative offices with effect from Monday, 4 March 1991.*

Why not put the important information first? *The two shipping administrative offices will merge on Monday, 4 March 1991.* Then you can explain your company's cost-cutting strategy to your heart's content.

If you want to draw the reader's attention to something, put it up front.

How might I achieve my purpose?

Simply conveying information is not that difficult. But if you are trying to move the reader to action, you have to be more resourceful.

If you are asking a favour, you should sound as obliging as possible; you should do everything you can to make it easier for the reader to oblige you.

If, on the other hand, someone owes you money and you need to reclaim that debt, it's no good using soft words in an effort to make yourself sound nicer. This is mere self-indulgence. The less direct and urgent you make the request, the less likely you are to get paid.

Here is a letter I was sent a few years ago after I had stayed in a hotel in the north of England. Read it and consider what the purpose of the letter was, and how effective the writer was in fulfilling that purpose. See if you can improve it. Then compare your effort with the suggested solution.

Dear Mr Morris

I am writing with reference to your recent stay here when you occupied room 136.

It came to light after your departure that you had not been charged for the drinks you consumed at the Terrace Bar on the night of 9 February totalling £10.70.

I apologise most sincerely for this oversight, but I enclose a copy of the bar docket signed by yourself and would request settlement of the above amount at your earliest convenience.

Once again my apologies and I trust this will not affect what I hope was an enjoyable stay.

Yours sincerely

Front of House Manager

Not too much wrong with this letter, you might think. But what was its purpose? Simple – to persuade the reader to send a cheque for £10.70 by return of post. And would it achieve this? Probably not. It is apologetic, it gives an impression of inefficiency, and it more or less pleads with the reader to make up for the hotel's shortcomings. Many people would ignore it, at least for a while.

Now consider how you would feel if you had received this letter:

Dear Mr Morris

When you stayed here on 9th February, we forgot to charge you for drinks consumed in the Terrace Bar that evening. I have enclosed a copy of the bar docket, which you signed. The total is £10.70.

This sum should have been added to the bill you paid the following day, and I am sorry to have to bother you now. Nonetheless I would be most grateful if you would send me a cheque for the outstanding amount. A stamped, addressed envelope is enclosed for your convenience.

We hope you enjoyed your stay, and look forward to seeing you again soon.

Yours sincerely

Front of House Manager

The stamped, addressed envelope is the clincher. There's nothing special about this second letter – no great literary skill required. It's just that the writer has thought about the two things that matter most: what he is trying to achieve; and how to achieve it by moving the reader to action.

What can get in the way?

All kinds of things can get in the way of writers communicating clear messages that achieve results. Wasted words and vagueness are two of those obstacles, of which the internal memos quoted earlier were examples. Easy enough, as we've seen, to avoid them by getting to the point quickly, and keeping your message as simple as possible. But other barriers to communication are more insidious. Jargon is one, but there's a more common problem even than that. It's the tendency most people have to imitate the familiar 'corporate' language that is all around them – language that is used to sound important rather than to communicate. If we're not careful we can all too easily be drawn into the sort of defensive writing that obscures meaning. Here's an example:

> *The key to the success of the new training programme was the utilisation of customer feedback to change the existing process to better meet customer needs.*

It's not incomprehensible, but it's hardly easy to read, is it? So much simpler to say:

> **The new training programme worked because we asked customers what they thought, then made the necessary changes.**

The original sentence is a classic example of nounitis – a fondness for abstract nouns (*utilisation, feedback, process, needs,* etc) which sound important but mean nothing by themselves, instead of verbs (*worked, asked, thought, made*), which move a sentence along, clearly explaining cause and effect.

We will explore such matters in greater detail in Part III

(nounitis is explained more fully in Chapter 9). But in the meantime, here's a tip that should help you avoid boring, impersonal corporate language. *Keep it simple.* Whatever the issue or subject is, think how you would explain it to a close friend, or to your mother. Then write that down. It will probably make surprisingly good sense.

2. *Who is Going to Read It?*

HAVING established what you are trying to achieve, you need to think carefully about who your reader or readers are, and how they are likely to react.

How do they see it?

Whoever wrote the following roadsign clearly failed to think about the reader at all:

**PHYSICAL WIDTH RESTRICTOR
REINSTATED**

The words on this sign make no immediate impression. When you take time to think about them, you can work out what they mean – but for a lorry-driver travelling at 30mph, this might take too long. The purpose of the sign is simple enough: to persuade drivers of wide vehicles to slow down, and make sure that they can squeeze through the gap. So why doesn't the sign say ROAD NARROWS, or specify what the width restriction is?

Let's pause for a moment and consider what happened here. We can imagine how the transport planners might have come up with this roadsign. They have to deal with various things that restrict the width of roads – bollards, the supporting arches of bridges, raised kerbs, etc. And for their purposes, the term 'physical width restrictor' may be a very meaningful one. In an internal memo it might be perfectly reasonable for one planner to alert another that a 'physical width restrictor' had been reinstated at a certain point. But, translated into a road-sign, the same phrase doesn't do the job. The writer, in this case, forgot to read the sign from the road-user's point of view. And who knows what the consequences might be? Poor communication might well cause a serious accident.

The lesson is simple: always put yourself in the position of the reader. In everyday life as in road transport, we cannot afford to get so wrapped up in our own priorities that we do no more than translate our personal thoughts into written messages, regardless of who might have to read them.

'You', not 'I'

There are countless other ways in which you can all too easily forget the reader. Take business correspondence. Whenever you write to a customer you should be asking yourself: does this matter to them? Am I addressing their concerns? Am I talking their language?

Compare these two openings from a bank's letter to a customer:

VERSION A:
I cannot trace any agreement between us for overdraft facilities and I shall be grateful, therefore, if you will arrange for an immediate remittance.

VERSION B:
You have no overdraft arrangement, so you should pay some money into your account immediately if you can. If you can't, please call me as soon as possible, and we can discuss your requirements.

Which is more effective?

Now look again at the words used. Version A uses bankers' language like 'facilities' and 'remittance'; Version B uses the customer's language. More significantly, in Version A, 'I' is used twice, 'us' once and 'you' once. Version B, apart from one mention of 'me' uses only the words 'you' and 'your'. It's a matter of courtesy, really. If you want the customer to act, you should address yourself to that customer as directly as possible. Use 'you', not 'I' or 'us' if you possibly can.

How do they feel?

It's easy enough, if you pause for a moment, to see things from the reader's point of view. Just think how *you* feel when you are a reader. If, for instance, you are a customer and you have made a complaint, the first thing you want to know is that your message has been received, that someone is listening. So if you are responding to a complaint, the first thing to do is to acknowledge the complaint or concern. There's nothing worse than receiving a response letter that completely misses the point you were trying to make. We'll look in detail at letters of complaint in the next chapter.

There are times when you have to make a special effort to understand your reader's feelings. And there is probably no greater test of reader-sensitivity than a letter of condolence. Actually, they're easier to write than you might think. But take care. The fact that you are dealing with a sensitive, emotional issue doesn't mean you should concentrate solely on writing from the heart, producing an outpouring of emotion.

For your reader's sake, think carefully. Why are you writing? You are writing to sympathise with your friend on his or her bereavement. This is not the moment to ask if she is coming to dinner next week, or to remind him about the forthcoming annual meeting – however urgent such matters might be.

Just think how you would feel, receiving a letter of condolence after the loss of a loved one. Would you be touched that your friend has taken the trouble of writing to you? Yes, you would. But would you want to be badgered about next week's social or business arrangements? No, you would not – at least, not just yet. So, as the writer of a letter of condolence, you've got to find another more appropriate way of dealing with day-to-day matters. Maybe you should give your bereaved friend a call next week.

Next important lesson. Don't use euphemisms, or words with which you are not familiar. This may be a letter of condolence, but you don't need to use the actual word, as in 'I am writing to express my deepest condolences.' You wouldn't use such formal words if you were face to face with your friend. So why use them now? Again, think how *you* would feel in his or her position. You would want to hear the authentic voice of the correspondent – not some borrowed verbal formulae suitable for solemn occasions.

So be yourself. Use words that come naturally. Why not simply write: 'I was so sorry to hear about your father's death'? Or, if you can get by without mentioning 'death' at all, even better. 'I was shattered to hear the terrible news about your sister.' But you needn't be shy of the word altogether. Your friend will be signing death certificates, putting death notices in the paper, making funeral arrangements. Don't tie yourself into knots trying to find a less harsh alternative if, again, 'death' is what comes naturally.

Now for the personal bit – a word or two about the dead person, how warm and humorous they were, how they made everyone feel as ease, how their work will be remembered. Whatever seems apt. Those of us who have received such letters know that there are only two things that really matter: first, that someone took the trouble to write; secondly, that they remember the person who died for some special quality, some kindness, or some particular achievement. Such things make the pain of bereavement just a little easier to bear. If you haven't suffered such a loss, you'll have to do your best to imagine how you might feel in those circumstances.

By all means offer to help in any way you can. But be realistic – there probably isn't anything you can do. And one thing you should avoid is telling your reader how they should handle their situation, or what they should be feeling. Think how *you* would feel. Would you want to be told to 'be strong', 'look on the bright side', or to 'surrender to your emotions'? This kind of advice, however well-intentioned, can seem intrusive and misplaced.

These are circumstances in which a sensitively written letter can make a real difference – and in which a thoughtless one can diminish the writer for ever in the reader's eyes. Literary skill has nothing to do with it. A good letter of condolence can be a masterpiece of brevity and simplicity. Here's a perfect example, a letter to Joan Morecambe after her husband, the great comedian Eric Morecambe, died in 1984:

My dear Joan

You have your private grief. We outsiders grieve too; but we rejoice that he lived.

We all loved him so.

Joy and Ronnie Barker

There's hardly any lesson to be learned from the letter of condolence that doesn't apply to every other kind of written communication, whether personal or business. With your overriding purpose in mind, you have to measure everything you write against the reader's likely reaction. And if you can't be sure about the reaction to a particular subject, it's probably safer to leave that subject out altogether.

There's just one pitfall about putting yourself in the reader's position. You mustn't presume too much. Never tell your readers what you think they are thinking. You could be quite wrong, and you could make yourself look very foolish.

PART II

The Right Content

3. *Letters*

THE RIGHT APPROACH, as we have seen, means thinking about what you are trying to achieve, and being constantly aware of how your reader is going to feel. Writing is essentially a conversation; it's just that you don't have the advantage of being able to monitor the reactions of the other person by looking at the expression on their face. When you write, you must try to imagine those reactions while simultaneously remembering that this is not just idle gossip, but a conversation with a purpose. Now we are ready to tackle the business of putting it all into writing – what to say and how to say it – in a wide variety of different contexts.

The Right Content will, of course, vary enormously depending on the task in hand. Let's look first at letters, both personal and business-related. Whatever the subject, there are three guiding principles that apply in virtually every case:

1. **Make a plan** For short letters, you can do this in your head, but for longer letters you might do well to jot down a few thoughts, then work out the best order in which to present them. It's not enough to have the right ideas; if a letter is not well organised it often won't work at all.

2. **Make a connection** Whatever the situation, whatever the story, the reader must be made to feel that this is of particular importance or relevance to them. If you have a personal connection with the reader, mention it; if you don't, try to 'put them in the picture' as soon as possible. Explain why you are writing to *them* and not

just anyone. Try to make the reader feel special.

3. **Stick to the facts** In letter-writing, the trick is to present the facts or issues in such a way that the reader will be drawn towards a certain conclusion. You want them to feel they have got there by themselves. (There is another powerful reason for sticking to the facts – you will be much better placed in the event of any legal dispute.)

A fourth principle that can apply in some cases is to include some specific incentive or inducement to move the reader to action – what sales people might call the 'deal clincher'.

Getting started

For business purposes you, or the organisation you work for, should have your own headed writing-paper. It's easy enough to create your own on a computer, provided you have a decent printer. If you can't, or you want to write a personal letter without your company letterhead, you should put your address at the top of the letter, preferably centred or flush with either margin (about an inch in from the edge of the paper).

It is normal business practice to put the name, title and address of the person you are writing to at the top of your letter, usually on the left-hand side, so that if the letter becomes detached from the envelope it is still absolutely clear to whom it is addressed. For example:

Anthony Jones
Managing Director
XYZ Company
15–17 Electric Avenue
Nottingham BC1 2YZ

It is not normally necessary to include Mr, Mrs, Ms or Miss in the address. The traditional way of addressing men is to put Esq (short for Esquire) after their name, and if you think your reader would appreciate it, by all means use it. But 'Esq' is gradually going out of fashion. Meanwhile, it is increasingly common to use 'Ms' for women – and quite useful in those instances when you don't know whether she is using her maiden or married name. But for the address at least, just the first name or initial and then the surname will usually suffice.

Next, your letter must have a date, inserted below the letter-head, above the letter itself. You should spell out the month, and use numerals otherwise. Whether you put the day before or after the month is optional, as is the use of the suffix *'th*. So 9 February 1998 and February 9th 1998 are equally acceptable.

Now, how should you address your reader? Not *Dear Sir/Madam*, if you can possibly help it. Just think how you feel when you get a *Sir/Madam* letter. You assume it is a mass-produced circular letter sent to many people. And if the letter-writer can't be bothered even to find out who they are writing to, why should you pay them any attention? *Sir/Madam* letters are prime candidates for the rubbish bin. So find out the person's full name if you don't know it and check the spelling along with their preferred title.

Forms of address

When it comes to addressing people with titles, there are umpteen complicated formulations and different conventions. If in doubt, refer to *Whitaker's Almanack* or, for greater detail, *Burke's Peerage*, or *Debrett's*. But here are a few hints that should help you get round the more common dilemmas.

To Sir Geoffrey Robinson, write *Dear Sir Geoffrey*. To his wife, write *Dear Lady Robinson*. But look out for those aristocrats who are Ladies in their own right. In this case, write *Dear Lady Mary*.

Dukes and duchesses should be addressed as *Dear Duke/ Dear Duchess*; envelopes should say *His/Her Grace, The Duke/Duchess of Wherever*. Marquesses, marchionesses, earls, countesses (wife or widow of an earl), viscounts, viscount-esses, barons, baronesses, lords or ladies of any kind should all be addressed as *Dear Lord/Lady XYZ*.

Most senior politicians (prime ministers, party leaders, secretaries of state) are privy councillors, and therefore entitled to the prefix *Rt Hon*.

If by any chance you have to deal with a member of the Royal Family, the best advice is to write to, or phone, the relevant private secretary – and be guided by that person from then on.

If in doubt, ask – even if it means asking the person in question how they like to be addressed. At least it shows you care.

Now to begin your written conversation. Use first names only if you have met the person, or established a warm telephone relationship and are already on first-name terms. Otherwise, *Dear Mr, Mrs, Miss* or *Ms*. Some women don't like being called Ms – so find out their preferred title if you can.

There are still quite a few people who like to see the *Dear...* handwritten, as a matter of courtesy. For those of us who habitually type or word-process our letters, it may seem strange to leave a blank at the top of the letter; but if you think it will be appreciated, then by all means leave a blank and handwrite the name in afterwards. This is a useful device when you are sending circular letters – to fellow-members of an organisation, for instance – to which you might wish to add handwritten notes to particular individuals.

Now, what does your reader need to know? Nine times out of ten, the first thing he or she wants is to be put in the picture. So it's up to you to explain, as quickly as possible, why you are writing, and in what context.

There is *never* any need to begin with *I am writing to advise you that...* Of course you are writing, just as the reader is reading and the clock is ticking – so get on with it! A lot of people worry that if they get straight to the point, they may sound rude. In most cases, this is just lack of confidence – and there is nothing more irritating to read than the apologetic language of the timid writer who feels obliged to wrap everything in verbal cotton wool.

Over the next few pages, we will discuss the vital ingredients of effective letter-writing in different contexts. Examples of model letters for many of these contexts are provided in Part IV, Chapter 13.

Sales

What does it take to sell something?

First, there must be a reason for interest – a benefit of some kind that is relevant to the reader. For instance:

Learn a foreign language in just three weeks

Protect your investments

Explore the opportunities of retirement

Secondly, there must be an appropriate product or service in which the seller clearly believes:

Growell Seeds – germination guaranteed; will grow in any soil

Advanced bridge coaching from the man who has taught hundreds of players to international standard

Undertakers for all occasions: thoughtful, discreet and 100% reliable

Thirdly, there must be a reason to act *now*, or buy this particular product rather than any other – a deal clincher, in other words:

Write now, and claim your free bottle of champagne

Special offer – this month only

Call free on 0800 XXXXXX to take advantage of this unique offer

This three-stage process should be sufficient for the most basic sales letters. And there's nothing wrong with being basic – the best sales letters are usually short and very much to the point.

Let's take a simple example – a jobbing gardener who has moved house and needs local work. Such a person might write the following circular letter to residents:

Rose Cottage
Rew Lane
Martinstown
Dorset
DT3 0QT

Dear householder

Do you sometimes need a hand with garden chores? I am a gardener, knowledgeable about plants, and expert in the care and maintenance of lawnmowers. Please give me a call on Martinstown 54321 – and if you're one of the first six callers I'll mow your lawn free of charge before the end of next week.

A letter like this deserves to succeed. The first sentence makes the connection – most people could use some help if they have a garden of a certain size. The second sentence swiftly establishes the writer's qualifications and commitment (references etc can come later). And the last sentence provides a good enough reason to give this particular gardener a call. Everyone likes getting something for nothing.

Other sales letters may be more complicated. Two further considerations are often crucial. The first is presentation – and here, the opening is always vital. If it doesn't grab the reader's attention straight away, the letter will probably go in the bin. One of the best ways of gaining attention is to give your letter a title, underlined and centred, eg:

<u>How to save money on car insurance</u>

<u>Your computer and the millennium – the facts</u>

<u>Seven chances to win £1m</u>

Other ways of gaining attention include:

- Capital letters, which must be used sparingly. SALE – LAST FEW DAYS or 50% OFF will catch the eye, but a profusion of capital letters can be a strain to read – one of the reasons why health warnings on cigarette packets are so little-read ...

- **Bold** or *italic* type

- Illustrations or cartoons

- Plenty of white space around the key message or messages

The second vital ingredient is some objective evidence of the quality or efficacy of what you are offering. Personal references are the best possible testimonials, so if you can quote a reference, do so:

> **Last week I replaced the ground-floor windows of your neighbour Mrs Lovett, and she seems very pleased with the result ...**

> **Your colleague Gillian Cox thought you might be interested in my service ...**

If you have no personal connection with your reader, but can provide some independent endorsement of your product or service, this can work equally powerfully in your favour:

> **'No software provider offers such a comprehensive after-sales service' – Bill Friendly, *Computer User* magazine**

In the absence of a genuine personal reference or testimonial, the seller must make the offer itself as personal as possible. No one does it better than the *Reader's Digest* in its regular Prize Draw. By explaining to the reader that they have been specially selected, as one of only two people in their street (and by repeating their name at judicious intervals in the sales spiel) the *Reader's Digest* persuades its readers – and that means *you*, Mr Morris – that they are uniquely privileged. They have a once-in-a-lifetime opportunity to win something for nothing; all they have to do is be prepared to buy a book or two on approval. An enormous number of people try their luck – and a certain proportion get hooked.

The one thing you must not do is bore your reader. If, for instance, you are trying to sell something mechanical, like a car, washing machine or personal computer, you should not get too technical. Most car-drivers don't think in terms of brake horsepower, units of thrust and carburettor modifications; but they do care about whether the car is easy to park, whether there's enough room in the boot and how many miles it does to the gallon.

Not every sales letter is initiated by the writer. Sometimes, a prospective customer will make an enquiry – perhaps as a result of seeing an advertisement. Now you are halfway towards your sale, so you don't need the hard sell. It's more a matter of reinforcing the reader's interest.

Sales letter: Example

X Y Z Bank
High Street, Chipping Bloxham, Oxon OX7 9BZ

Mrs F G Jones
23 Honeypot Lane
Chipping Bloxham
Oxon 0B7 3TA

10 April 1998

Dear Mrs Jones

You telephoned this office yesterday to enquire about the mortgage offers mentioned in our recent advertisement. Having heard about your circumstances, I have no hesitation in recommending our young family mortgage.

This scheme is specifically designed for people like you who

plan to take time off work to have a baby and therefore need to reduce your outgoings for a period. It offers you a 2.5% discount (that means a third off the current 7.5% mortgage rate) for up to two years during the first seven years of your mortgage. So, for instance, you can pay a reduced rate for the year immediately following the birth of your baby.

The Young Family Mortgage offers:

- A flexible discount that takes account of your family plans

- The 'lowest current rates available' (*What Mortgage?* magazine)

- No arrangement fee

Finally, if you take advantage of this offer now, we will enter you in a one-off competition: there are three Rover Metros to be won (each with child-seat, of course) for the first three names picked out of the hat among the families who take out a Young Family Mortgage by 1 August. So please fill in the enclosed form, and we will help you get your new family off to the best possible start!

With best wishes

Yours sincerely

Karen Armstrong
Mortgage Administrator

The introduction makes clear that this is not a standard piece of direct mail. The content is specifically aimed at the reader. The bullet points emphasise attractive features. And finally, the competition provides the impetus on the reader to act *now*.

Exercise: Imagine you have bought a bakery, and taken on most of the existing staff. You are equipped to bake many different kinds of bread, as well as cakes, pastries and the like. Compose a brief one-page circular letter to customers of the old bakery (assume you have names and addresses) announcing your reopening, and incorporating your own deal clincher.

Compare your efforts with Model Letter 1 in Chapter 13.

Introduction

A letter of introduction is a sales letter of sorts. You are selling yourself, or the products you represent.

If you can claim a genuine personal contact, mention it straight away: 'I met Ray Evans last week and he suggested I contact you.' A familiar name will be sure to catch the reader's eye, and gives your letter a better chance of being read.

Perhaps you are introducing your business, in which case you want to give a positive impression. Get to the point as quickly as possible, and try to empathise with your reader. 'Since Eezikleen closed down last year, South Elmsall has had no local window cleaner. Our company, C-Thru, aims to fill that gap...' Then you can go on to explain what your company offers in more detail. You should still be able to get it all on to a single page.

Other letters of introduction may well be more open-ended, requiring a softer kind of sell. Perhaps you simply want to arrange a meeting, in the hope that something comes of it. It would be foolish at this stage to look much beyond the meeting.

If you are introducing someone else, the first essential is the personal touch. Is there a good reason why you should be writing to this particular person? If there is, mention it straight away.

You said you were always interested in young talent...
Do you remember saying you could do with a research assistant?

You will then need to give some basic information about the person you are introducing, and this is almost certainly one of those occasions when you should stick to the facts. Be enthusiastic by all means: 'I'm sure you'll enjoy his/her company.' But don't try to oversell the person; far better to leave that to them. The fact that you have taken the trouble to write at all should count in their favour.

Introduction letter: *Example*

M & M Widgets Ltd
Haymarket House, Carlisle, Cumbria CA9 8TT

Roger Wright
Wright's Engineering Co
Wright House
Pinwinnie Business Park
Perth

Dear Roger

This is just to introduce our new marketing manager, Sally Palmer, who joined us last week. Sally has plenty of experience in light engineering, having worked for ABC Widgets from 1995–7. She is intelligent and energetic; perhaps more unusually for someone with a sales background, she is a good listener! She will be in touch with you soon to find out what we might do for you over the coming months, and I hope you will be able to make time to see her.

Yours sincerely

Gerald Davis
Managing Director

Exercise: A business friend of yours has just organised a management buy-out and wants to hire a new accountant. Write to him introducing your own accountant (who happens to have handled one or two MBOs).

Compare your efforts with Model Letter 2 in Chapter 13.

Reference

This is more than a simple letter of introduction. You are standing, to some extent, as guarantor for the basic honesty and trustworthiness of anyone for whom you agree to act as referee. So only provide a reference for someone you genuinely wish to recommend. If you have any substantial doubts about a person, say you don't feel qualified to write a reference.

Having decided that you are prepared to act as referee, highlight the positive qualities that you have personally noticed, explain in what capacity the person has worked for you and for how long, and make a clear recommendation. Don't make extravagant claims, particularly if the person concerned is applying for a job in a new area of responsibility.

Reference letter: Example

Fuller & Associates
125 Parliament Street, London SW1

Anthony Scott
Personnel Director
PR Consultants
500 The Strand
London WC2

31 May 1998

Dear Mr Scott

I have no hesitation in recommending Zoe Pitcher as a personal assistant. She worked for me in this capacity for nearly two years, and I found her competent, trustworthy and helpful. I can't remember her missing a day's work, and she was always prompt and well turned out. Feel free to give me a call if you require any further details.

Yours sincerely

Celia Barnforth
Partner

When you give a letter of reference or recommendation, it is usually at the request of the person concerned, and they would not normally expect you to write a long letter. The curriculum vitae should take care of the essential details. Nonetheless, what you leave out can be as important as what you put in – particularly if you never mention key issues like honesty, competence and reliability.

Exercise: Compose a letter of reference for an office cleaning company run by a personal friend. Bear in mind what any prospective client will most want to know about: efficiency and trustworthiness.

Compare your efforts with Model Letter 3 in Chapter 13.

Invitation

We shall not deal here with formal invitations, as for weddings: Mr and Mrs L Jones request the pleasure etc. The form for such invitations is well established; if you are unsure, consult *Debrett's* or *Whitaker's*, available in any public library.

More complicated are invitations where you have a little discreet selling to do. This kind of invitation letter can easily fail to make its mark, either because the event is not sufficiently enticing, or because it does not seem particularly relevant to the reader.

If you really want someone to come to an event, the surest way is to address them personally.

Invitation letter: Example

New World Technology
19–21 St Peter's Street, Chelmsford, Essex CL6 2RM

Jane Francis
Marketing Director
Chambers & Longman
29 Roman Way
Colchester, Essex

19 July 1998

Dear Jane

On 13 May, we are celebrating the company's 20th anniversary and we would be delighted if you could join us for dinner. We are inviting only a select band of friends and most valued customers. Guest of honour will be the former Test cricketer and renowned entrepreneur Albert Twistlethorpe, who is one of the most entertaining after-dinner speakers I have heard.

You are invited for 6.30pm, so that you can see a brief demonstration of our new software package, which should be of special interest to you. It would be great to see you and Gerald there. Please ring me or my secretary and let us know if you can come.

With best wishes

David Trent
Managing Director

A letter like this is clearly personal, and will be harder to refuse than a formulaic invitation. Your ulterior motive is that you get to show your captive audience your new gizmo when you hope they will be feeling warm towards you.

If you really want someone to come, then the onus is on you to explain why the occasion will be of particular appeal:

This should be right up your street
I can promise you and Diane a thoroughly enjoyable
evening

At other times, it may be more difficult to make a powerful case as to why someone should accept your invitation. No one is immune from flattery, however, so if you have a chance, be sure to mention that you saw them on television, enjoyed their speech on such-and-such an occasion, read their interview in the house journal, or read their report on XYZ Project. Or, more simply:

We have only invited our favourite clients
Everyone here is dying to meet you

Exercise: Imagine you are the head of an organisation such as the Round Table, looking for a speaker for your annual dinner. You can't pay this person, but you can offer a good dinner, appreciative company and a bed for the night. Assume it's someone you recently heard delivering rather a good speech at the CBI's annual conference. What would be your opening paragraph? Just jot something down, then compare your effort with the opening to Model Letter 4 in Chapter 13.

Application

This could be an application for a job, a loan, or membership of a society or professional body. It is both a sales letter and a letter of request. As such, it will certainly require a personal touch – which is often most difficult to handle when the subject is yourself.

The first question to ask yourself is, what does your reader want? Secondly – and closely connected – is the question of what you can offer them.

Do as much homework as you can beforehand. What kind of members does this society currently possess, and what kind does it want to attract? What kind of person normally qualifies for this sort of loan, and can you provide the necessary credentials? What kind of company is it that you are applying to join? What is its ethos, what distinguishes its best people, and are you likely to fit in?

If you're not sure about the answers to any of these questions, you probably shouldn't be writing an application – not yet, anyway. Telephone the company/organisation first, then tell them you are planning to send in an application and see if you can find out more.

Your application letter must be confident and straight-forward. State your interest, your qualifications, and, briefly, why you believe you qualify for whatever it is you are seeking. Enclose any relevant information: a curriculum vitae, references etc.

Application letter: Example

James Dyson
7 Rose Dawn Cottages
Pipers Lane
Wantage
Oxon
WA6 2HL

Mayfair Fine Arts Society
300 Park Lane
London W1

15 September 1998

Dear Mr Jones

I have long wanted to become a member of the Mayfair Fine Arts Society, for which I believe I now qualify.

I have exhibited my paintings at galleries in Oxford, Guildford and Richmond, and I enclose a review from the *Richmond and Twickenham Times* which made favourable mention of my work.

I have visited the club on several occasions over the past year, and have always felt very much at home. I enclose

supporting letters from two club members.

I hope you and your fellow members of the membership committee will look kindly on this letter of application.

Yours sincerely

James Dyson

This letter should have the right combination of modesty and deference to flatter the reader. Most clubs and societies take themselves pretty seriously, and expect anyone applying for membership to be in awe of the institution. So this is an occasion when you don't blow your own trumpet, but show appropriate modesty and try to appeal to what you hope is your reader's generous and inclusive spirit.

Most organisations – banks, for instance, and professional bodies – will have application forms, but in certain cases, letters such as this may be all you need.

A job application, by contrast, probably requires rather less deference and more obvious enthusiasm:

I honestly believe I have just the qualities you are looking for
Please give me the chance to show you what I can do
This is precisely the kind of challenge I relish

But restraint is still important. By all means mention your good qualities – your organisational ability, your efficiency, or whatever. But don't sound boastful. Your prospective employers want to know why you are applying for this job, your qualifications and experience, and your likely ability to do the job in question. But they won't be expecting all the answers in one letter. They will probably only be looking for enough evidence to make them think it worth inviting you for an interview. So don't try to make an open-and-shut case. Be true to yourself, and write in the style that comes most naturally to you. Think about the structure and content – making the thrust of your letter as relevant to that particular employer as you possibly can.

Exercise: Imagine you've seen a job advertised for which you think you would be ideally qualified. (Let's assume that the salary and conditions are suitably attractive, too.) Now write a short letter of application, with which you will send your curriculum vitae. Then have a look at Model Letter 5 in Chapter 13, and see if you've managed to strike the right note of being competent and confident, but not too pleased with yourself.

Request – products, services, favours, fund-raising, payment

When you are asking for something, your tactics will vary enormously depending on what you want. This section deals with requests for information, products or services, favours and money – including requests that turn into demands, as when bills become overdue.

If you want information, you must be as specific as possible – whether you are paying for it or not. A cricket supporter, for instance, might enquire of Warwickshire County Cricket Club: 'Please can you tell me how many runs Brian Lara scored for Warwickshire over the 1995–6 season, in all competitions?' In this instance, the last three words are especially relevant, as separate records are kept for the four-day county championship games and for the various one-day tournaments.

The same applies to many everyday commercial transactions: a request for products, for instance, will often best be achieved by using a list.

Request letter: Example

ABC Co Ltd

15 South Street, Bickley-on-Tyne, Durham BT7 8BL

Ordering Dept
Office Equipment
34 High Street
Gateshead

12 August 1998

Please send the following by return, and charge our account accordingly:

- **20 A4 document folders (Ref no: AB 103)**
- **100 HB pencils (Ref no: ST 249)**
- **1 grey filing cabinet (Ref no: GP 543)**

If there is any problem with these orders, please telephone …

Yours sincerely

John Spalding
Purchasing Manager

If you are paying for a service and you know exactly what you want, spell it out clearly at the beginning. Later on, you might need to put some pressure on your suppliers, and you will be much better placed if they have made a written commitment to a deadline. If they think you are asking too much, this is their chance to argue. If they accept the proposition you have outlined, the onus is on them to deliver:

We aim to complete the building work by 20 March, and we must have the interior decoration completed by the end of the following month. Can you meet this deadline?

Now for a very different kind of request. You are confused, or uncertain, and need help or clarification. In essence, you are asking a favour, so you need an altogether different tone:

I am afraid I don't quite understand ... and I would be most grateful for your help

This is an appeal to your reader's better nature. It would surely be churlish to refuse such a polite request.

When you really want something, there is a temptation to spend too much time explaining your problems, or your reasons for writing. Far more important to make it clear to the reader that they can make a real difference, and to make it as easy for them as possible.

With a fund-raising appeal, for example, it is a mistake to overdo the all-out assault on the heartstrings. Of course a story of human tragedy or deprivation should move your reader. But journalists and politicians use the rather cynical phrase 'compassion fatigue' to describe the threshold we all have for sympathising with other people's misfortunes. From the reader's point of view, there comes a point at which horror and natural sympathy give way to the realisation that the more terrible a situation is, the less likely it is that their contribution will make any difference. We all know there isn't much we can do about war or famine on a global scale. That is why more and more charities are trying the more personal approach – 'Adopt an orphan', 'Adopt a granny' or 'Adopt a wild animal' – so that readers are able to imagine what their contribution is providing for a specific living thing; they can feel that they are actually making a difference.

Exercise: Imagine you have been persuaded to accept the chairmanship of your local school's Parent/Teacher Association. The school wants to build a badly-needed new gymnasium and has just received approval for a lottery grant of £25,000, conditional upon the school raising a similar amount on its own behalf. After various fund-raising events, the school is still £5,000 short. Building is due to start in a few months, but only if the money can be found quickly. Compose an appropriate appeal letter to parents asking for immediate funds, then compare your effort with Model Letter 6 in Chapter 13.

Chasing letters

Other requests for payment may be couched very differently.

In Chapter 1, we saw how a polite letter accompanied by a stamped, addressed envelope could be used to induce someone to pay a bill they had not previously been asked to pay (the hotel letter). With habitual late payers, it may be necessary to be less gentle.

When chasing debts, you must be calm, methodical and determined. Ultimately, whether you are a company or a sole trader, you must be prepared to take legal action.

If you have not been paid within the period laid down in your terms and conditions, find out who is the responsible person and write a polite but firm reminder, headed with the relevant invoice number (and account number if applicable).

Chasing letter: Example

Alan Hudson Roofing
Chappell Road, Blackburn, Lancs BL6 4OF

Charles Nash
Accounts Department
XYZ Company
Archibald Road
Blackburn

1 July 1998

Dear Mr Nash

Reminder: Invoice No 1598
[this heading may appear immediately above or immediately below the 'Dear...']

We note from our records that we have not yet received payment for Invoice No 1598, for £765, for repair work on the roof of your premises. That work was completed on 29 June, and the invoice was delivered to you that day. It is now three days past the final date for payment stipulated in our invoice.

Please would you arrange for this invoice to be settled without further delay? If you have a problem or query, please contact this office as soon as possible. And if your payment has crossed with this letter, we are sorry to have bothered you.

Yours sincerely

Geoff Milligan
Accounts Manager

If nothing happens for another three weeks or so, try something like this:

Charles Nash
Accounts Department
XYZ Company
Archibald Road
Blackburn

23 July 1998

Dear Mr Nash

<u>**Second Reminder: Invoice No 1598**</u>

It is three weeks since we wrote to you, reminding you of this unpaid invoice, and we have yet to receive a reply. Our terms are clearly stated, and you have never queried them.

We do not want to have to take this matter to your managing director, far less involve our lawyers. But we shall have no choice if this bill remains unpaid for much longer.

We look forward to hearing from you by return.

Yours sincerely

Geoff Milligan
Accounts Manager

If this doesn't work, you will have to go higher.

Exercise: Write to the managing director of XYZ Company explaining why you will be obliged to involve lawyers if a final deadline is not met. Compare your efforts with Model Letter 7 in Chapter 13.

You may wish to vary your tactics slightly according to the client and their previous payment record. But keep the language direct and simple. Even if the letters do follow a standard formula, try not to make them sound formulaic – or they may well be ignored until a really angry letter from a really angry person is received.

Complaint

This is one instance where tactics and self-control are vital. If you start off with all guns blazing ('I have never been so shabbily treated in my life…' 'How dare you treat your customers in this fashion?…' 'If you think I'm going to take this sort of thing lying down…'), before you know it you will have burned your boats and promised to take your business elsewhere – in which case, what is the point of writing to complain? If your letter has any effect you won't be able to benefit.

On the other hand, you certainly don't want to appear apologetic, mild or diffident, or the reader will assume that you can be easily fobbed off with excuses.

The key elements of every complaint letter are as follows: you must set out the facts as objectively as possible, suggest undesirable consequences if nothing is done to repair the damage, and – crucially – give the reader the opportunity to repair the damage. Restraint is all-important. The following letter is a good example of a complaint that worked (it began with a phone call to check the name of the person responsible for handling complaints).

Complaint letter: Example

Robert Wilson
Marketing Director
PQR Wine
12 Hope Street
Hopetown

12 December 1997

Dear Mr Wilson

Two weeks ago I went to the East Street branch of PQR Wine to take advantage of your special offer of seven bottles of Montana Lindauer for the price of six. As I know and like this wine, I intended to order two cases, one for myself and one for my mother-in-law. Unfortunately, they were out of stock at this particular store, but they took my order and promised to let me know when more stock arrived. In due course, I received the call to tell me that the wine had arrived. But when I went to collect it, the sales assistant refused to give me the four extra bottles to which I presumed I was entitled. He said the offer was only valid while stocks lasted. I protested, but the assistant clearly felt he was acting in line with instructions. A queue was forming behind me, so I left the shop with my two cases, determined to take the matter further.

This is surely an extraordinary way to apply a special offer. It wasn't that your central stocks of this wine had been exhausted, merely that this particular branch had temporarily run out. The special offer was the main reason I ordered the wine in the first place. When I ordered the wine, no one told me the offer would no longer apply.

I have been a good customer of PQR Wine for the past five years, and would like to continue to buy wine from you. But if you cannot satisfy me on this point, I shall have to take my custom elsewhere.

I look forward to hearing from you.

Yours sincerely

Sebastian Follett

This letter clearly did the trick, because the complainant received four £10 vouchers by return – rather more than the value of the original offer. *Restraint is the key*. There is no suggestion in this letter that anyone was acting maliciously or negligently. It's a reasonable complaint, clearly and coherently put, and the easiest thing is for the marketing director to agree with it and gain a satisfied customer, who will surely think better of PQR Wine as a result, and remain a good customer for many years to come.

If the same letter had become overheated, emotional, expressed outrage at the behaviour of the shop assistant, or made unrealistic threats, the marketing director might well have concluded that he could do without this particular customer.

Exercise: You are the owner of a video store, and one of your regular suppliers has failed to provide you with the items you ordered (the last order was for ten copies of *The Full Monty* and five copies of *Titanic*). This has caused you some embarrassment with regular customers who placed orders you could not fulfil. It is also the third time in two months that this supplier has let you down. You don't want to sever relations, but you want immediate action, plus some recompense. Write an appropriate letter to the managing director, Reg Garside, whom you have met a couple of times. Compare your efforts with Model Letter 8 in Chapter 13.

Condolence

The letter of condolence was discussed at some length in Chapter 2, as a prime example of the need for reader-awareness. But the main scenario given there was for someone writing to a friend. Occasionally, you might find it necessary to write a letter of condolence to someone you do not know.

Whatever the circumstances, a letter of condolence need fulfil only two simple tasks: first, make the connection with the reader, and use language appropriate to that reader (formal with someone you don't know); secondly, say something kind about the deceased. If in doubt, please refer back to Chapter 2.

Exercise: You have just called a close business contact to confirm a date next week for a game of squash (or a concert, or whatever social or sporting fixture seems appropriate) only to learn that he has not come to work because his father has died. You now feel you should write a letter of sympathy. In the back of your mind, however, is the question of what to do about the squash/concert date. Should you keep the booking open, cancel it, ask someone else, or what? Over to you. Compare your efforts with Model Letter 9 in Chapter 13.

Information

Providing information is simple: put the most important news first, then include anything else that might be relevant to your readers.

Here, the headquarters of a large chemical company has written a circular letter to suppliers.

Information letter: Example

TDK Chemicals
PO Box 6, Liverpool 11

M Rogers
Sales Director
XYZ Widgets
Anytown

5 September 1998

Dear Mr Rogers

<u>Purchasing Policy</u>

We have received a number of enquiries at this office recently, which we have referred to our plant purchasing managers. This letter is simply to clarify our purchasing policy.

Following last year's reorganisation, purchasing decisions have been almost entirely devolved to our three plants in Huddersfield, Lincoln and Wolverhampton. Please contact the purchasing manager at the relevant plant to discuss orders, delivery and payment.

The only time the Liverpool head office might become involved in purchasing matters would be in the event of a problem or dispute.

With our best wishes for the continuation of a successful business relationship,

Yours sincerely

Purchasing Director

Information should be neutral; a responsible company will treat good and bad news with equal candour.

Good news is easy to deal with. But with bad news – disappointing half-yearly results, for instance, or redundancies – there is a temptation to try to soften the blow by explaining all the reasons first. This is a bad idea. As the readers wade through the rationale, they sense there's bad news on the way, and they resent what they see as your making excuses.

If, on the other hand, you give the bad news first, there is nowhere to go but up. You can then explain that it was unavoidable, that others have been worse hit, and that there are certain options still available to those affected. In this way, readers may be persuaded to go away with the feeling that 'it could have been worse' and that you have at least been fair and honest – which is some kind of victory in the circumstances.

Exercise: Your company's half-year results show a trading loss of £93,000, compared with a profit for the previous six months of £255,000. Demand for your products/services fell but there were other factors, too. The company had to install a new software program to handle all accounts and inventory (at a cost of £200,000); and there was a fire at your main warehouse which caused a delay of several weeks in fulfilling orders. In the coming year, you hope that the new systems, allied to a staff cut of 15%, will rapidly improve profitability. Write a one-page letter to shareholders fully explaining the position. Compare your efforts with Model Letter 10 in Chapter 13.

Accepting/declining invitations

Accepting an invitation is easy; the type of invitation dictates the manner of the response. Often a phone call may suffice. A formal invitation, however, requires a formal response. Either: 'Stephen Jones thanks Mr and Mrs Bloggs for their kind invitation to..., and has great pleasure in accepting.' Or: 'Thank you so much for your kind invitation to ... I shall be delighted to come.'

With a more personal invitation from a friend or a close business contact, a more personal response might be acceptable: 'Lovely to receive your invitation this morning. I will be thrilled to come. See you there!'

Declining need not be any more difficult. If it's a formal invitation, decline as follows, depending on the degree of formality of the invitation. Either: 'Rupert Morris thanks Mr and Mrs Bloggs for their kind invitation, but regrets he will be unable to attend.' Or: 'Thank you for your kind invitation to… Unfortunately, I have a previous engagement and, sadly, will not be able to come.'

With a more personal invitation, you should try to be as friendly and conversational as possible. You might use phrases like: 'What a shame…' 'There's nothing I would have liked better…' 'Unfortunately, we just can't get out of…'

Exercise: A friend and business contact has asked you and your spouse to come to her firm's 50th birthday party, which she is organising. You are really sorry to miss it, but you have to be at a sales conference in Amsterdam. Write with your apologies. Compare your efforts with Model Letter 11 in Chapter 13.

Rejection or refusal

Whether you are responding to a complaint, a request, or an application, your task is straightforward: to convey a negative message while avoiding distress and providing as much encouragement as possible.

As when informing people of bad news, you should not delay the blow any longer than necessary. But if you are rejecting a suggestion or complaint, politeness dictates that you acknowledge the suggestion first.

Rejection letter: Example

Jacobson Publishing
22 Bedford Row, Covent Garden, London WC2 6NR

Dr Jonathan Hewitt
24 Hall Place
Carshalton
Surrey

30 July 1998

Dear Dr Hewitt

Thank you very much for sending us your manuscript, *Illness in the Workplace*.

Unfortunately, we cannot publish it in its present form. We feel that it is simply too technical for the business market. At the same time, I feel you have several important and interesting points to make, and that it would be a great shame if you were not eventually to find a publisher.

As I see it, you have a choice. You clearly have the qualifications to write a serious academic work; that is not a field in which we publish. You could therefore approach a specialist publisher.

On the other hand, if you would like to move in the opposite direction – setting the book more clearly in a business context – I would be very interested to meet you to discuss a re-write. If this is a course you would like to pursue, please telephone this office to arrange a meeting.

Whatever you decide, thank you for sending us *Illness in the Workplace*. We wish you the best of luck with it.

Yours sincerely

Sabrina Firth
Editor

Rejecting a job application is much harder. Again, get the negative out of the way as quickly as possible. Don't keep your reader in suspense, raising their hopes only to dash them later.

Tell them they failed to make it on this occasion, explain why, as politely as possible, and go on to highlight their positive attributes, before concluding with advice on what they should do next. In this way, a rejection letter can actually set someone on the right path. A few years hence, that person might even come back to you with the qualifications or experience they lacked on that first occasion.

Exercise: You have interviewed 15 people for jobs as management trainees, when there were only two vacancies. Among those you are now obliged to reject is Christopher Thorpe, a bright and pleasant young man whom you would like to bear in mind for the future. Write him an appropriate rejection letter. Then compare your effort with Model Letter 12 in Chapter 13.

Refusal

A letter of refusal, like one of rejection, should break the bad news as tactfully as possible while attempting to retain the goodwill of the reader. If you begin by sympathising with your correspondent's demands, you will give them a sense of being on their side, which should make them more receptive to the bad news to follow.

Refusal letter: Example

J & S Watches & Clocks

St Pancras House, Redditch, Worcs. PE3 2NZ

Henry Ansell
99 Green Lane
Sheffield

11 November 1998

Dear Mr Ansell,

Thank you for your letter of 24 June. I can imagine how disappointed you must have been to realise that your newly-purchased watch was not, as you had believed it to be, waterproof.

A watch that is described by a manufacturer as water-resistant is guaranteed to withstand such things as being caught in a shower of rain or splashed in the course of washing-up. But this is by no means the same as being waterproof – like a watch of the kind worn by deep-sea divers. It is somewhat like the difference between a light-weight raincoat and a sailor's oilskin.

In the case of the watch you bought, the instruction leaflet explains these matters quite clearly – although I appreciate that very few people choose to read such information in detail. Since the goods were not misrepresented to you, I am in no position to offer you a refund.

I do sympathise, however, and because we would very much like to retain your custom, I am happy to offer you a 25% discount on your next purchase at this shop.

I hope you will understand that this is the best I can do for you in this instance.

Yours sincerely

John Waterstone
Customer Services

If appropriate, thank your reader for their request or enquiry:

Thank you for enquiring whether KMO Ltd might wish to advertise in your magazine
We appreciate your interest in our company

Express some regret at having to refuse:

Unfortunately, this isn't possible
I'm afraid we cannot help you on this occasion

If you want to avoid severing all ties with whoever you're refusing, the trick is to craft your letter in such a way that the refusal itself becomes almost a secondary issue. This might be achieved by adhering to the points above, adopting a courteous manner and – most important – going on to suggest an alternative line of action to the one your reader had in mind, or recommending another contact:

Perhaps my colleague, Mr Jones, would be interested
Maybe our head office would be able to help
Have you considered writing directly to the manufacturers?

Exercise: You own a small gift store. Respond to a customer who has written requesting a refund for an item which they decided, a week after purchasing, wasn't suitable. Point out your policy, which you display clearly in the shop, of not giving refunds unless goods are faulty or have been misrepresented. Offer them a credit note or straight exchange, as long as they have the receipt. Compare your efforts with Model Letter 13 in Chapter 13.

Resignation

When the time comes to leave an organisation, you may well be relieved; the chances are you will have been thinking of handing in your notice for some time. But don't leave on a sour note – you never know when you might need help from former colleagues. Whatever your reasons for leaving may be, it can only reflect well on you if you leave with a good grace and some kind words for those you leave behind.

As a matter of form, you should mention precisely when you propose to leave.

I submit my resignation, effective 2 June 1998
I will be leaving on 2 June 1998

If you can give your reasons without causing offence, do so:

Considering the financial benefits and potential of the position, I couldn't afford to turn the offer down
I feel I need a fresh challenge

Finally, make some reference to the good points of your soon-to-be-ex-employer:

My association with RJ Associates has been a happy and rewarding one
I have greatly enjoyed working with/for ...

Resignation may also be an opportunity to make a point, perhaps get something off your chest – provided this does not involve the settling of a grudge. A gracious letter of resignation might read along the following lines.

Resignation letter: Example

Middlemarch Football Club
Eliot Road, Middlemarch, Lincs. MH3 7HA

2 February 1998

Dear Supporter

It is with great regret that I have decided to resign as chairman of Middlemarch FC Supporters' Club. I have held the chairmanship for three seasons now, during which I am proud and happy of the fact that our membership has risen

from 1,400 to 1,900. The club itself looks poised for greater things in the coming season, and as my business commitments were bound to make it impossible for me to continue after September, I thought it better to resign now, and give you a chance to elect a successor in plenty of time for the new season.

I am extremely grateful to all those who have helped to make my time as chairman a rewarding and memorable experience. I would particularly like to thank Ray Fossett, who gave me great support with the Stamp out Racism campaign. I'm happy to say that coloured players from our team – and from visiting teams – have noticed a great improvement in crowd behaviour in this respect. Let's keep up the good work.

Finally, my thanks and appreciation for the loyalty of every member of the Middlemarch Supporters' Club. I shall still be around next season, joining the rest of you in hoping for the best for our team. They deserve our support.

With every good wish for the future,

Yours sincerely

Mark Hughes
Chairman

Exercise: Imagine you are leaving your current job, with some relief, but with no desire to settle old scores. You have had no opportunity to see your boss in person, but must write a letter of resignation immediately. You might like to compare your effort with Model Letter 14 in Chapter 13.

Reprimand

A letter of reprimand is a real challenge in terms of content. How do you tell someone that their work is not up to scratch, that they are taking too much time off, that they are letting the company down?

In the first instance, you will probably wish to deal with the matter in person. But there are times when your company's disciplinary code makes a written reprimand not only appropriate but essential. As with a letter of complaint, you should avoid inflammatory language and state the facts as simply as possible. You don't want to be sued for libel! If you intend that any further breach of discipline should lead to dismissal, you should say so. As with the letter of complaint, you should offer the reader the chance to make amends.

Reprimand letter: *Example*

Walker & Co

Green Fields Business Park, Stevenage, Herts. ST5 47Z

Ella Stephens
67 Letts Road
Stevenage
Herts

26 January 1999

Dear Ella

You reported for work at 9.35am yesterday – the third day this month that you have been late for work without having given any prior notice. This has caused considerable disruption and inconvenience, both to your manager and to your colleagues.

Your terms of employment are quite clear, and require you to work from 9am to 5pm. As you well know, these hours can only be varied by permission from your head of department. In the circumstances, I have no choice but to issue this official reprimand.

If you are late again without any explanation, you will be liable to be summarily dismissed. I hope it won't come to that, and you will make a serious effort to arrive on time – or at least telephone if some mishap threatens to make you late.

This reprimand will remain in force for six months. Provided there are no further incidences of lateness, it will then be expunged from your record.

Yours sincerely

Alan Spicer
Personnel Department

Other letters of reprimand may be more complicated, but should follow the same pattern: stating the facts and explaining possible consequences without being unduly personal or threatening.

Exercise: Two members of staff have complained about one of your marketing executives returning from lunch drunk, making lewd conversation, and being noisy and disruptive. This is not the first time you have received such a complaint, and you now feel you must issue an official warning. You want to make clear to the person concerned that you don't want to lose them, but you will not tolerate behaviour that upsets other members of staff and disrupts their own work. Draft a letter, then compare it with Model Letter 15 in Chapter 13.

Dismissal

Once the decision has been made to dismiss someone, the news should always be conveyed in person. The subsequent letter is purely to establish the legal facts.

There are legal implications to cases of redundancy or dismissal; specific company procedures need to be followed before a letter can be sent and you should always seek legal advice if in doubt as to your rights. Once you are sure of your position, your letter should be factual and to the point. Avoid lengthy explanations and personal comments other than simple courtesies.

In the event of a redundancy that you genuinely regret, you can write:

It is with deep regret that ...
I'm sorry to have to tell you ...

You could end on a positive or encouraging note:

We wish you every success in finding a new position

If you genuinely believe in the abilities of the reader you could write:

I have no doubt that you will soon secure a suitable position with another organisation

Provided you are certain of your legal position, you may also wish to offer praise, or a reference:

Your performance and enthusiasm have made you an asset to the company
I will certainly provide a good reference if you need it

Dismissal letter: Example

Harmony Public Relations
12 Temple Street, Bristol BS2 5OX

Richard Twiggett
17 Clifton Road
Bristol BL3 6TM

24 June 1998

Dear Richard

On 12 April, I wrote to you issuing an official warning about being drunk in the office. Yesterday, on your return from lunch at 3.25pm, you abused one of the secretaries, fell over a desk, damaging a lamp and some files, and were subsequently sick in the corridor on your way to the lavatory. In line with company policy, I have no choice but to dismiss you for misconduct.

Your employment ceases forthwith, and you should contact

Geoffrey Benson, Personnel Manager, for your P45 and other documentation.

Yours sincerely

James Browning
Managing Director

Apology

First of all, say how sorry you are; this is the most disarming tactic at your disposal:

> **I'm so sorry. I just can't imagine how I could have forgotten to post that letter**
> **I was sorry to hear that you were unhappy with...**

Once the apology is out of the way, you can start to think of ways in which you might remedy the situation:

> **Can I pop in and fix it on Tuesday?**
> **The enclosed voucher will enable you to buy a replacement at any of our branches**

Many successful business people will tell you that a complaint requiring an apology is a unique opportunity to bind a customer to you for a long time. And they are quite right: where otherwise will you have the chance to confront an issue on your customer's behalf, win a battle for them, provide them with a personal service that goes far beyond the initial customer/provider contract, and make them feel that somebody cares about them and understands their problems?

> **I have spoken to the staff concerned and warned them as to their future conduct**
> **I have drawn your complaint to the supplier's attention, and they have promised to improve their checking methods**

Your apology letter may be only a small part of the process of satisfying the customer. Or it may be the key element. Either way, it should do the following:

- Respond directly to the specific complaint
- Explain what you are going to do about it – including compensation, where appropriate
- Provide some indication of your commitment to quality
- Sign off with appropriate words of apology and good wishes

Here is a standard letter devised for a leading superstore to respond to complaints about the condition of food.

Apology letter: Example

XYZ plc

Fresh Foods House, Midland Way, Luton, Beds.

Mrs S Jones
15 Uplands Close
Bedford
BE7 9QA

27 March 1998

Dear Mrs Jones

Thank you for contacting us on [date]. I was sorry to hear about your unfortunate experience with ...

I have passed on the details of your complaint to the supplier concerned so that he can investigate and take the necessary remedial action. In the meantime, please accept the enclosed £... in compensation.

We make every effort to ensure that our products are fresh and in the best possible condition. Our technical department selects foods according to very stringent specifications, and our quality assurance technologists regularly visit suppliers and depots to check that standards are being maintained. Clearly, on this occasion there was a slip-up, and we shall do our best to ensure that nothing like it happens again.

Thank you for bringing this matter to our attention. Once again, my apologies for the inconvenience, and I hope you will continue to enjoy our products without any further mishaps of this kind.

Yours sincerely

Harold Spencer
Customer Relations

Whenever you find yourself in a weak position, remember that evasive language only makes you sound weaker still. After a full and frank apology, you should move on as quickly as possible to show that you are prepared to take positive steps to remedy the situation. Even if you can't change the system or be sure that similar mistakes will not recur, you can at least show that you've done your best. That way, you should earn your customer's respect, perhaps even gratitude.

Exercise: Imagine you work for a bank and someone has been given incorrect information about their overdraft. As a result, this customer suddenly and unexpectedly found himself unable to draw out money. The complaint is reasonable, the facts are true, and the customer has clearly suffered considerable embarrassment. Write an appropriate response on the chief executive's behalf, then compare your effort with Model Letter 16 in Chapter 13.

Signing off

Before you sign a letter, make one last check that you have left a clear impression, persuading your reader to react in the way you intend. Even if there is no deal clincher at the end of your letter, you might wish to encourage your reader to look forward to a meeting or other future event, or simply leave them with a warm glow.

For instance:

I look forward to seeing you on the 21st
I shall call next week to arrange a meeting
We appreciate all your help in resolving this situation

Avoid the over-used ending: 'If you have any further queries, please do not hesitate to contact me.' If you've done your job properly, there shouldn't be any further queries. Besides, do you really want to encourage your reader to take up even more of your time?

The truth is that 'please do not hesitate to contact me' has become an automatic sign-off. It may once have sounded friendly and obliging; but now, through over-use, it has come to sound insincere and impersonal. Besides, it is not something you would actually *say*, and conversational language always sounds more accessible and friendly. So, if you want to end on this note, you might write: 'If you need to clarify anything, please give me a call. Or: 'If anything is still unclear, ring me on the number at the top of this letter.'

Now how should you sign off?

The best bet, in almost every case, is 'Yours sincerely'. 'Yours faithfully' can be saved exclusively for those rare, formal letters that begin 'Dear Sir/Madam'. A lot of people nowadays use 'Warm regards', 'Kind regards' etc; the test is to consider the reader. If they send 'Kind regards' to you, or you think it is the kind of amiable expression they would appreciate, then by all means send them back. If you favour 'Yours truly', that is not going to offend anyone. 'Best wishes' are always acceptable. 'Yours', by itself, is much more informal, and should only be used when you are on first-name terms with your reader. Other more casual expressions – 'All the best', 'See you soon' etc – depend entirely on your relationship with the reader.

The PS (postscript) is much loved by marketing departments because it stands out from the rest of the text, so usually gets read. But it is not a device that should be used habitually. A good, crisp letter comes to the point quickly, covers all the relevant facts and shouldn't need a PS. But by all means use one if you want to add some vital detail that you are determined to lodge in the reader's mind.

4. *Reports*

IF YOU WANT to learn how to write reports, study the professionals: read a daily newspaper. Reporters are trained to provide their readers with the essential facts in descending order of importance, so that the reader sees the headline, then reads the first paragraph and knows more or less what the story is, before deciding whether to read on for further details. Newspapers work on the basis that nobody reads every detail of every single news story, so readers need the best possible signposting in order to make their choices.

If only people in business did the same. The truth about business reports is that a lot of the intended readers don't actually bother to read them. Some don't give them a second look; some just look for the summary and ignore the rest. Others skim-read. Even the few who actually read the whole report would usually find the experience much easier and more rewarding if the material were more thoughtfully presented.

The precise form depends on the kind of report involved. If you are simply recording the minutes of a meeting, for instance, there is little scope for innovative layout or illustration, and you are certainly not required to produce conclusions or recommendations. But even at this most basic level of report-writing, you want to be sure that you are compiling the minutes in the way your readers want; it is in nobody's interests for you to record irrelevant details, or to present your material in a format that is dull or difficult to follow.

This chapter provides a step-by-step guide to writing the kind of reports that get read, not ignored. Whatever the task or subject matter, Step 1 is the place to start.

Step 1. Assessment and information-gathering

Ask yourself why you are writing this report, and for whom. What is it really designed to achieve? Far too many reports are compiled according to a long-established formula with little or no thought given to the end result. Have you fully understood the brief? What will your readers want/expect to learn from the report?

Even with something as straightforward as a meeting report, you have at least two choices: are you expected to use shorthand (and, perhaps, make a tape-recording) and write up the full minutes as a reliable and detailed record of an important meeting? Or will it be sufficient to summarise the main points in the order in which various speakers made them? If, for instance, it is merely the first exploratory meeting of a working party, it is unlikely that anyone will want detailed minutes; rather, they will want a quick reminder of the main points raised – ideally on a single sheet of paper. But with a more crucial meeting at which issues of importance are raised and debated at length, it will be in everyone's interests that the proceedings are recorded in full.

There are three main types of report, and each requires the reporter to gather certain types of material.

1. Meeting report or minutes

This should always include the following:

- Time and place
- Names of those present, or of those participating
- A true record of proceedings
- Notice of next meeting

If you are providing full minutes, your job is to note each speaker in turn, and compile an accurate record of what they say. A lot of speakers talk in sentence fragments, often littered with grammatical errors; it is not the minute-taker's job to record these literally, but to convey the sense of what the person says. Interruptions – whether from other participants in the meeting or from the public gallery, or from external causes such as sudden thunderstorms or power cuts – should be recorded, but not in any detail. Your task is to record the meeting, not the events surrounding it.

Hansard, the official record of parliamentary proceedings, is a model for minute-takers; an extract is provided in Chapter 14.

Apart from remembering to read through and check for errors, the minute-taker's task is a relatively simple one. Other kinds of report require more forethought, planning and organisation.

2. Analysis report

This could include anything from a situation report or update to an in-depth feasibility study. But essentially it is a report in which the onus is on the writer to take as objective a view as possible, while drawing out the implications of every item of information. It therefore requires that you gather information under headings like these:

- Objectives and scope of report
- History or background
- Description of situation and relevant factors
- Implications and options
- Summary of prospects (may also be inserted at beginning as executive summary)

Everything depends upon the brief you are given, and the subject you are tackling. In many business reports, financial calculations will be important; in police reports, witness statements may contain the most relevant information. And so on. But whatever the subject matter, you need to be clear about your brief. And what is your deadline? Are there any budget constraints? If you're not sure, check.

3. Report with recommendations

This covers much of the same ground as the analysis report, but requires the reader to go further and make a recommendation or recommendations. Sales proposals, feasibility studies and tipping reports come under this heading. All the information in the report is marshalled with one clear objective or decisive course of action in mind.

Information needs to be gathered in much the same way as the analysis report:

- Objectives
- Background
- Evidence
- Assessment of options
- Conclusions and recommendations

An executive summary is usually put at the front for the reader's convenience.

Once you know exactly what you're supposed to be doing, assemble all the printed material you have – notes, research documents, press cuttings, graphs, tables, completed questionnaires etc. Read through it; this is the equivalent of the news reporter going to the cuttings library. The more information you have to start with, the more likely you are to ask the right questions – and to answer them.

If you think it necessary to do a substantial amount of original research, you'd better check with your boss first. It might be advisable to write a short memo, explaining how you are approaching the task, and how long you expect to take. There's an element of self-protection here, and why not? If you get a nod, then you can reasonably assume that you are on the right track; and it will be that much more difficult for anyone to complain that you compiled the report too hurriedly – or took too long – or included too much, or too little, detail. If your proposed approach is queried, or vetoed, then you may well have saved yourself a good deal of wasted effort.

Assuming there is research to be done, you must be disciplined about it. Explore all the obvious information sources – libraries, colleagues, databases, the Internet – but don't let yourself be distracted by non-essential information. You may well have to speak to a number of interviewees – in which case you should limit yourself to a maximum number of interviews, client meetings, site visits, or whatever is needed.

If the list of potential interviewees seems worryingly long, perhaps you should consider compiling a questionnaire, or circular letter. These can be extremely useful, enabling you to conduct a wide canvass much more quickly. You can also use the questionnaires to find out who is willing to be interviewed, and who is not. This is one area where business and journalism are very different: for a journalist, reluctant interviewees can be more intriguing, because they may have something to hide; but for business purposes, if people don't really want to talk, an interview is probably a waste of time for both of you.

Finally, even at this early stage, you should be thinking about illustrations for your report, which may look terribly uninviting if it is just page after page of typed paragraphs. Do you have any useful tables, graphs or pie-charts? Is there any scope for using photographs, or even cartoons? Do you have any press cuttings that could be used as panels? If there is no scope for graphic illustration, perhaps you can use some case studies or real-life stories to illustrate the various key issues. These always help to create pictures in the reader's mind, and provide essential light relief from what might otherwise be tediously abstract and theoretical material.

Here's a short checklist for the basic report requirements:

- Have I got enough information, from enough relevant sources?

- Do I have a realistic schedule, budget and deadline?
- Do I really know what this report is supposed to accomplish?

If the answer to any of these questions is 'no', go back to your source or boss, put yourself in the position of your prospective reader, and make sure that you have done all you reasonably can to ensure the practical value of your report.

Step 2. Planning

Assuming your information-gathering is more or less complete, your next step should be to plan the report in skeleton form.

Look carefully through your material, and highlight key passages. Consider your main subject headings (eg terms of reference, objectives, background, meetings, present situation, assessment of options, findings, recommendations, cost, appendices etc) and mark sections of material to be used under those headings. You might find it helpful to number your headings. Then, when you go through background material, you can mark it with a 3, or whatever the appropriate number is for that category of material. When you come to your findings, mark them with whatever the appropriate number is. And so on.

Scribble, highlight, rearrange. Different-coloured highlighters can be useful. Gradually your report skeleton, or outline, should be taking shape. And the whole process should be giving you a clear idea where you are going before you start writing in earnest.

Let's take an example – a surveyor's report and valuation on a three-bedroomed terraced house with garden. After including time and date of visit – and weather – the report might well contain the following headings:

1. Front elevation
2. Rear elevation
3. Ground floor
4. First floor
5. Second floor
6. Attic and roof
7. Basement
8. Garden (front and rear)
9. Approximate value

But there are other possibilities. An introductory paragraph commenting on the house and its surroundings might well be appreciated: 'Overall impression' might be the heading. After all, a three-bedroomed terraced house in a mining village where the pit closed down ten years earlier is a very different proposition from a three-bedroomed terraced house in Mayfair.

Another appropriate heading would probably be 'General condition'. Most surveyors' reports, at least on property of a certain age, appear to consist of a series of criticisms – warped doors, weaknesses in the floors, deterioration in plasterwork, patches of damp etc. But the reader will gain a very different impression if there is a paragraph explaining that these imperfections are only to be expected in a house of this period, and that this particular property is in fact in much better shape than most of its neighbours. Whatever the report covers, it should almost always be set in context.

Let's consider another scenario. An annual report for a chemicals company might begin with the chairman's message (the equivalent of the surveyor's 'overall impression'), then cover the various parts of the business (equivalent to the various parts of the house):

1. Agriculture
2. Pharmaceuticals
3. Industrial chemicals
4. Chemical intermediates
5. Fibres and polymers
6. Research
7. Environment
8. Employee training and development
9. Community work
10. Health and safety

Could some of these logically be bracketed together to avoid duplicating information – health, safety and environment, for example? These are matters on which the writer will almost certainly have to take advice. It will depend how the company wishes to project itself this year, which areas of the business it wants to highlight. But it is vital to have a clear, balanced outline before you start writing the report.

Finally, you should consider at the planning stage whether

there isn't some subject, a case study, for instance, which you would like to include in some detail, but which, as it is almost entirely illustrative – demonstrating your point rather than making it – might be better dealt with in an appendix.

Exercise: Imagine you work for a bank and you want to compile a report on a country to which you are planning to send a team of analysts. In the long term, your interest is in assessing the economic potential of the country and the prospects for investment. That country is Argentina, and this is a brief summary of some of the main points of information:

Argentina is probably the fastest-growing economy in Latin America. Covering just over 1m square miles, it has a population of about 33m, mostly speaking Spanish. Almost half the total land area is pasture for cattle, with beef, mutton, wool and farm products accounting for at least 80% of its exports. The BSE crisis has left Argentina unscathed, because its cattle have enough grass to eat all year round. Indeed, beef exports are rising rapidly. Forestry and wine are small but growing concerns. In trade with Britain, Argentina exports about four times as much as it imports. But its major trading partners are the US, Brazil and Germany. It has promising oil reserves, and minerals like copper and gold which have only recently begun to be profitably mined; the rights to exploit oil, gas and mineral deposits belong to the provincial governments, which control commercial leases.

Politically, it seems more stable than in the days of the military junta which embarked on the Falklands War in 1982. Privatisation and other economic liberalisation policies have helped to reduce inflation to negligible levels. But unemployment is rising uncomfortably. There is widespread corruption, in politics and business, but the banking system is sound. The financial infrastructure is seriously underdeveloped, but foreign investors are beginning to reshape industry. Elections are due in 2000, with a defeat for the current government likely.

From this information you can construct a rough outline for a full report, deciding on suitable headings and identifying any topics on which you need to carry out extra research. Draw up the outline, divide the text up under your chosen headings and then make a note of the extra details you would need to write a full report. Compare your efforts with the full report, with headings, in Chapter 14.

Step 3. Executive summary

You might think you should leave the summary till the end, when you will be in possession of all the arguments and facts. But do yourself a favour and have a stab at it before you begin to write the report. Consider the professionals again: most reporters, as soon as they have a certain amount of information, begin to think in terms of how they will project the story – what the main thrust of it will be. And that's exactly what an executive summary should express.

The executive summary is so called because it is intended for busy executives who may not have the time or inclination to read a long report, but need to know about the key issues highlighted or recommendations made. What they want is to be able to see at a glance what the report covers and what its main findings are. Then they can decide whether they want – or need – to read the rest. A good executive summary – not one that fills several pages, please – is one of the best tests of a good report. If the summary reads well, it is proof that your report has a clear and convincing message, and readers will be encouraged to read on, to explore the finer detail of what you have to say.

From your own point of view, writing a summary now will also give you a much clearer idea of where you are going. In fact, if you are unable to write one at the planning stage, perhaps you should reassess the whole report. After all your research, you should know by now what the main issues are, and what your conclusions and recommendations are going to be. If you change your mind about these in the course of writing the report, you can always rewrite the summary at the end. It isn't set in stone.

Take this real-life scenario. A financial director wants his company to consider contracting out its office cleaning services before an impending office move, and has commissioned one of his managers to look into the matter. The following is the manager's executive summary at the front of a six-page report:

> **Cleaning of our offices is currently carried out by an in-house staff of 28, at an annual cost of £141,000. The best contract cleaning quote received so far envisages 20 staff, at an annual cost of £93,000 – an immediate saving of 34%. Despite the cost of laying off the current staff, the shift to contract cleaners looks to be in the company's interests. But for legal, financial and operational reasons there is little to be gained by changing cleaners before the office move.**
>
> **I therefore recommend the following actions:**
>
> - **Commission both XYZ Cleaners and our current in-house cleaners to provide a detailed report on the cleaning required at the new premises**
> - **Assuming that XYZ's quotation is cheaper, give notice of termination to our current cleaners, while inviting those who wish to work at the new site to contact XYZ, which has promised to look sympathetically on applicants from our present offices**

This brief summary gives all the essential information – certainly all that a busy executive needs to know in the short term. And it immediately puts in the picture people like the personnel director, trade union representatives and others who will doubtless want to read the details of the full report.

Exercise: Imagine you are contributing to a restaurant guide giving at-a-glance summaries of restaurants in the West End of London. The guide is aimed at restaurant-goers who want basic information before choosing where to eat. The following is a review of Sutherlands, a now defunct Soho restaurant, written in 1988. Edit it down to no more than 100 words, including all the essential information the reader of the guide will need.

Sutherlands (45 Lexington Street, London W1. Tel: 0171 434 3401.) 'Soho Newcomer of the Year', and at 15 out of 20, clearly the highest-rated new entry in the *Good Food Guide*. Open midday to 11pm Mon to Sat. Closed Sundays. Wheelchair access. Vegetarian options available. Smoking or non-smoking areas. No music.

Sutherlands is certainly different. There can't be another restaurant that goes to such lengths to discourage passing trade: the name above the door in lower-case lettering, the windows paint-washed so it looks as if it's closed for re-decoration.

As we walked through the door we were mobbed by a manager and several waiters fighting for possession of my hat and coat. I had heard the service was good.

Our table was in the far corner of the long, split-level dining room. In the front half was a sporadically raucous group of *Phantom of the Opera* fans. The only other occupied tables belonged to men in suits, one of whom would persuade his colleagues from time to time to raise their glasses to admire the colour of the wine before swilling it thoughtfully round their mouths.

While the aperitifs were brought, we took in the decor, on which a lot of money had clearly been spent. The walls are stippled pale egg-yolk, the hidden lights point upwards. A dark blue carpet makes the light on the lower walls bleak. There are no pictures, just peculiarly hideous mirrors. The stained-glass panels in the ceiling are no more attractive.

But what we really came for was the food, and in this we were not disappointed.

There is a surprise menu at £37.50, but there is no shortage of interest in the two-courser for £21.50. Starters are stunning, with a pasta parcel of lobster, mussels and truffles in a langoustine sauce just having the edge over my warm oysters glazed with a lightly curried sauce (actually more reminiscent of hollandaise) on a bed of artichokes.

Main courses were almost bound to be a disappointment after this: I could have done with more than two slivers of daurade and red mullet, and less of the unexpected celery underneath; a combination of venison, hare and pigeon with walnuts, truffles and a rich but delicate sauce was much better. Puddings at £4.50 looked enticing, and the English farmhouse cheeses were a fine mixture of tastes and textures.

After the house wines at £8–11, prices rise steeply, but a bill of £92 (which could have been £80 if we had stuck to a single bottle of house wine) was far from excessive for food of such a standard.

A valedictory visit to the Gents, however, re-awakened my earlier irritation at the austere and pretentious decor. The signs on the doors were barely decipherable sketches of a man and a woman. If I didn't have good eyesight I could easily have blundered into the wrong one.

This determination to make a statement via the decor is anything but relaxing, and the excellence of food and the obliging smiles of the staff served only to emphasise the laboratory-like bleakness of the surroundings. There'll be a counter-revolution soon, with red plush furniture and gilt-framed pictures. I can't wait.

Quite a lot to squeeze into 100 words. But just consider the main points: in a nutshell, the writer loved the food but didn't like the decor... Have a go, then compare your effort with the shortened version in Chapter 14.

Step 4. First draft

Now start writing the first draft. Try to stick to the headings you've created, but if they don't seem to be working, be prepared to change the headings, or change their order. To make sure you are on the right track, keep reminding yourself who is going to read the completed report. And keep writing; you can't afford to get bogged down in the search for perfection at this stage. This is, after all, only a first draft.

Apart from completing the executive summary, which will probably end up at the front of the document, your first task will be to set the scene (under headings like 'Objectives', 'Terms of reference', 'Background' or 'History'). You will need to answer – in writing – some or all of the following questions:

- When, why and by whom was this report commissioned?
- What is the relevant historical background?
- Who has been involved in discussions or meetings to date?
- Why is this an important matter, and what are its implications?
- What are your sources of information?

The chances are that some of your readers will know much more about the subject than others. Just because your boss – or whoever commissioned the report – knows certain things, you can't assume that everyone else does. So make sure you explain any technical details fully. If this seems laborious, you could always create an appendix for those detailed passages that will be of special interest only to a certain section of your readership.

Don't use jargon if you can possibly help it (see Chapter 9 on Plain English). Imagine how you might explain the situation to your mother: that way you should be able to come up with something clear and comprehensible. If it seems too simplistic, you can always refine it. But don't change the wording merely to sound more official, more pseudo-authoritative, more 'corporate'.

Much of a report, particularly in its early stages, is a journey of explanation. Keep reminding yourself of that. Whatever it is, explain it. You've got to keep your readers fully informed.

Having covered the historical background and the current situation, you will want to move on to some sort of assessment of current options. This has to be more than your personal opinion. Muster all the evidence you can, name your sources if possible, and *keep explaining*. Be as specific as you can: give examples.

If you are expected to include recommendations in this report, you will in due course find yourself moving from explanation to persuasion. You are a bit like a barrister making a case: you've outlined the facts, and now you need to call as many witnesses as you can to support your case. Primary sources, press reports, tables and graphs may all serve as witnesses for your purposes. And just as a barrister will keep referring back to 'ladies and gentlemen of the jury', so you must keep relating everything you are saying back to the reader. You may not write 'Dear Reader' in the course of a report – but you need to keep thinking it.

When you have presented all the evidence, you need to work towards your conclusions or recommendations. Don't strive for effect; if you honestly can't decide between two courses of action, then present two choices, briefly explaining the case for each.

Above all, by the end of your report, you must feel that you have enlightened your readers. You haven't conducted this entire investigation only to leave them more confused than they were at the beginning. Your job is to shed light.

Remember:

- Put the reader fully in the picture
- Keep explaining
- Make a good case
- Be clear

Now, if you can, leave the report overnight, or turn your attention to something else for a while.

Step 5. Presentation: second draft

After a suitable pause, take a fresh look at your report from the reader's point of view. Is it easy to read? Does it flow? Is it logical and well laid-out?

This last point is vital. You might think that the most essential ingredient in a report should be its content: Is the quality of research up to scratch? Have the important issues been properly investigated? Does it have some useful conclusions or recommendations? And, of course, these are vital questions. But the most deeply researched, intellectually rigorous report will be useless if it doesn't actually get read by the people who matter.

When you consider that, in some organisations, the only way to gain the attention of the chief executive is to present an idea in the form of 'storyboards' – the advertising industry's equivalent of a strip cartoon – the importance of presentation becomes obvious. Your job is to present your words in such a way that they are attractive to read and appeal to your prospective reader.

Here are a few points to bear in mind about layout.

Of people who pick up a newsletter:

- 100% read headlines and photo captions
- 70% read sub-headings, bullet points, underlined or bold items and quotations taken out of the body text
- 5–30% read the text itself

What applies to newsletters applies in much the same way to reports, letters and faxes. So try to present your information in the most accessible; attractive way possible.

Here are some ways of making your writing easier and more pleasurable to read:

- Use short words, sentences and paragraphs
- Use wide margins to create more 'white space'
- Use plenty of headings and sub-headings
- Use graphics or illustrations where possible

- Make sparing use of capitals, bold type and underlining.
- Use lists, with either numbers or bullet points

The presentation of a report will depend, above all, on the client's wishes and expectations. If the report is commissioned by an executive who simply wants quick answers, it may well be sufficient to produce something short and to the point, with a brief executive summary, consisting of only a few pages, with bullet points and eye-catching information panels on every page – all held together with a single staple in the top left-hand corner.

If, on the other hand, the client is paying several thousand pounds for your report, he will want something that looks good, with a laminated cover, a table of contents, and perhaps 20 or 30 pages of well laid-out copy, interspersed with illustrations, tables and information panels.

In either case, page numbering is essential – and please don't put the number on the left-hand side, where it may disappear under a staple or other form of binding. Paragraph numbering is less essential; the sheer repetition of numbers can become tedious. But there are circumstances in which it is useful to be able to refer to numbered paragraphs. Let the client's wishes be your guide.

Choose an appropriate title for your report. Make it as short and relevant as possible. Resist any temptation to emulate tabloid headline-writers by trying to write something witty or shocking. Aim for what is factual and memorable. Put your name on the cover, with your office address and phone number (if appropriate) plus the date on which the final draft was completed.

For other presentational niceties, see Style Points in Chapter 11.

Step 6. Check and send: final draft

Check for accuracy, and for any possible legal implications. You should never make a comment about any living person or company that you cannot substantiate, nor should you make commitments you may not be able to fulfil.

Have you acknowledged your sources? This is hardly the occasion on which to commit to paper effusive thanks to your spouse or secretary, but if you have drawn extensively from one particular source – such as an earlier report by a company colleague, or one expert interviewee – it would be both courteous and appropriate to mention this.

Do you need anything else: footnotes, glossary or bibliography? Probably not, if you have managed to acknowledge your sources as you go along. But if you have used a lot of unfamiliar technical terms, it might be worth considering a brief glossary at the end.

Can you deliver your promises? Are there any possible misunderstandings? Have you fulfilled the brief? If in any doubt, don't be too proud to get a second opinion. But don't be browbeaten into watering down your report. You don't want to end up with a useless document full of vague assertions and hedged bets.

Finally, where are you going to send this report? Does it need a covering letter?

If you've followed all six steps with care, this should be a powerful report – a weapon at your disposal. So don't just send it off and wait for reaction – that would be like building a fighter plane and leaving it on the runway for the enemy to shoot at. Make sure the right people get it and read it – or at least that they read the right bits. If there's someone you know will be interested in a particular passage, call that person, or send it to them highlighted, with a covering letter. And if you anticipate opposition to your recommendations, seek out likely allies, so that you are better placed to win the argument. You've put a lot of work into this project. Make sure it works for you.

5. E-mail

The joy of e-mail

In the brave new world of the Internet and electronic mail, the global high-flier no longer needs pen, paper and briefcase; the personal computer can take care of just about all requirements. If you need to have frequent conversations with colleagues hundreds of miles away, in different time zones, you no longer have to wake each other up in the middle of the night. You no longer have to leave messages that might be intercepted or misunderstood by another member of staff, or jotted down on a piece of paper and mislaid. You can simply type out your message on your computer (or get your secretary or assistant to do it for you), send it to the appropriate electronic mailbox, and your reader or readers can check and read their electronic post before tucking into their morning cornflakes.

Ideas can be exchanged without any pressure being applied. People can send and receive e-mail in their own time, without the time and expense of buying paper, envelopes and stamps and making trips to the letterbox. Why, it's even more efficient than speaking to someone face to face! After all, in a typical conversation, one person can lose out at the moment when the other is talking, or interrupting; some of the best ideas don't get voiced, or get forgotten moments later. By contrast, in e-mail conversations nothing of the immediacy and spontaneity of thought need be lost, and you can make sure you are saying exactly what you want to.

It's great for your clients, too. You can update them electronically in minutes rather than days, send them news, quotations and briefings as they happen, or ask them crucial questions, without ever needing to worry about interrupting them at inconvenient times.

Consider the advantages:

- You save time and money – a few touches on mouse and keyboard are enough to send your message

- You don't need to contact the person face to face, so no appointments, no interruptions, no waiting time

- No matter where in the world you are, an e-mail message will get there quicker than a letter, quicker even than a courier, except over very short distances

Reasons to be careful

Now let's look at the disadvantages. When you write a letter, and put it in an envelope addressed to a particular person, you can be reasonably confident that it will be read by that person and that person only, unless they deliberately choose to share the contents with anyone else.

With e-mail, you just can't be sure. In the first place, the medium is inherently insecure: unless your message is encrypted, it can easily be intercepted. Secondly, various things can go wrong in transmission – it's easy to make tiny mistakes with e-mail addresses, the server sometimes gets overloaded, there are occasional software incompatibilities, and of course computer breakdowns are not unknown. These hitches are commonest when you are making new connections; once you have established a regular e-mail connection, the system is pretty reliable.

There is a third caveat which is perhaps the most important. The Internet is a brand new medium, and new users are making up their own customs and standards as they go along. Attitudes are quite different. Electronic communication is fast, spontaneous and, in some respects, anarchic. It is not a medium for considered judgments, in-depth discussions and exchanges of weighty confidential information. Whereas someone would hesitate before handing a personal letter on to a third person, they might unhesitatingly press a few keys on their computer to pass an entire message on to others who might be interested only in certain aspects. Or they might extract a section and incorporate it in a fresh message to be sent somewhere else. The electronic medium makes recycling of information so easy that whatever you send by e-mail, you can never be quite sure where it is going to end up, or in what form.

Finally, e-mail is not a satisfactory medium for communicating long documents. These are a strain to read on screen, and although they can be printed out, this usually results in the loss of some enhancements, so that the document looks unprofessional and is tedious to read. Besides, printouts may not be possible if you are on an aircraft or in a taxi using a laptop computer.

So before we rush into sending electronic mail, let's consider the disadvantages again:

- Less than 100% reliability
- Lack of security
- Depth of discussion limited by culture of spontaneity
- Unsuitability for long documents

How to send e-mail

When you send an e-mail message, you name the intended recipient of your message by giving their e-mail address. You fill in your own name unless your software does this for you. And you fill in the 'subject' line. This is important: someone who receives a large number of e-mail messages every day will often find it necessary to be selective. Just as one might leave the occasional bill or circular unopened for a day or two, people will leave non-urgent e-mail messages until they have a spare moment. But if something is headed 'Change of meeting date' or 'Urgent, please contact...', they will almost certainly read it straight away.

So make good use of that subject line. If it is not an urgent message, do your reader a favour and make it clear: 'When you have time…' If it is urgent, take care to use words that you know will act as triggers to your reader: 'Project X latest' or 'JV's response at last'.

For example:

FROM: Edward Stagg <StaggEC@glasgow.ac.uk

TO: clarity@globalnet.co.uk

DATE: 23 May 1998

SUBJECT: Writing courses

Take care not to use wide margins – your text might disappear off the recipient's screen, making it almost impossible to read. As a general rule, you should keep lines no longer than 80 characters.

How to write e-mail

At its best, electronic conversation can draw people together as effectively as if they were in the same open-plan office. But it only works as it should when people are prepared to let the barriers down, forget old hierarchies and exchange ideas in a truly creative and cooperative spirit. You should have nothing to fear; your best ideas, once conveyed by e-mail, become evidence in your support. If someone tries to pinch your idea, you can produce evidence that you thought of it first.

The principles of good writing remain unaltered. After all, any e-mail message is liable to be transferred to paper – so it needs to satisfy the same criteria. The differences in approach are, to a great extent, tactical, depending on whether you are writing for internal or external consumption.

Informality is usually the key to getting the most out of e-mail. If you write to people in a conversational tone, you will probably encourage them to let down their defences, too. This applies internally:

Jeff

Look, I'm really sorry, I can't make it on the 16th because I've promised to say a few words at Gillian's leaving do. I guess I'll see you the following Tuesday for the planning meeting. Can we grab a bite afterwards?

And externally, as with this message from an export agent to his client:

Rick

Great news. Megalift can do exactly what you asked. But they want to charge £16,000, which seems a bit steep to me. I said I would consult you and come back to them. I was hoping it wouldn't cost more than £10,000, but I guess I won't be able to beat them down that far. I'll do my best, but I doubt I can get it down to less than £14,000. What do you think?

No complications, no frills. Just facts, questions, essential conversation.

Writing for different readers

The spontaneity of e-mail is both its strength and its limitation. Because people tend to use it informally – to chat, to exchange ideas without thinking too deeply about the implications – it makes it all the more essential that, when you have really important messages to convey, you think carefully before you use it.

There is a big difference between sending an e-mail message outside your firm, and communicating internally.

Internal messages

With internal mail, the important thing is usually to communicate ideas, misgivings, queries or observations before they go out of your head.

Exercise: A colleague, Gina, has just made a presentation about reorganisation plans in the event of an anticipated merger. You thought her presentation was very persuasive, but had to leave before the end. Now something's just occurred to you: what if you go ahead with buying the new software you've been discussing and the merger doesn't happen? Would you still want the software, or would the company's requirements change? Gina's travelling now, and you don't know where to reach her over the weekend. You and she must discuss this on Monday before the board meeting. Send her an urgent e-mail message. Compare your effort with the Model E-mail in Chapter 15.

External mail

With external e-mail, you need to take just as much care as you would if you were sending a fax or letter. You need to ask yourself: what will my reader(s) think? what reaction do I want? And, therefore, what should I say and what shouldn't I say? Your message is fulfilling exactly the same function as a letter, and courtesy therefore dictates that you frame it in much the same terms.

You may well decide to begin your message 'Dear X' and end with 'Best wishes'. 'Yours sincerely' is probably too formal for an e-mail message, but there are no absolute rules here, so you will have to judge for yourself what will go down best with that particular reader. It might be, for instance, that your e-mail is going to someone whose secretary is in the habit of printing all such messages out – in which case the more like a formal letter it is, the better. It is up to you to find out as much as possible about your reader before you write.

Exercise: A prospective client has given you a pile of documents relating to a new product – a collapsible bicycle – and wants you to produce a detailed marketing strategy, for which he expects to pay. There is the chance that if he likes the strategy you have outlined, he might give you the job of marketing the product. Having read the available documents, you would like to discuss the project with a colleague, and envisage spending two and a half days on a strategy document, for which you would like to charge £2,500. Write him an e-mail to that effect, and compare your effort with the Model E-mail given in Chapter 15.

One warning. Whether it's an internal or external message, you may need to be careful when dealing with different cultures. A blunt negative, for example, can cause great offence to a Japanese. So if you work for a large multinational company, just remember who your readers might be, and try to keep your writing as clear, crisp and neutral as possible.

Sending documents

Regular users of the Internet will know that the basic message-sending mechanism is limited to short paragraphs of normal prose. Variations in setting, typefaces or even £ or $ signs may not be accurately reproduced at the receiving end. So if you want to send a formatted document, particularly one with graphics, you will need to send it as an 'attachment'.

A brief reminder, then, of some of the best uses of e-mail:

- Use e-mail for brainstorming – top-of-the-head ideas that you are happy to share with the widest possible audience
- Use e-mail to ask questions – you might get the answer from an unexpected quarter
- Keep messages short, pointed and factual
- Be careful before using e-mail to convey opinion, gossip or news that is capable of various interpretations

E-mail etiquette

As befits a new form of communication, e-mail has developed its own etiquette. With thousands of new people connecting to the Net every day, this etiquette is not yet known to everyone, and is still evolving.

As you become more familiar with e-mail, you will notice that people who use it regularly adopt a unique tone of voice that is direct, friendly and conversational. When you depart from that tone of voice, it comes as a shock. Using capital letters in the main text of your message, for instance, is generally frowned upon; it is felt to be equivalent to shouting.

Because e-mail users want to emulate the pattern of normal conversation as closely as possible – e-mail is most like having a slow-motion, long-distance chat – they have a peculiar way of adding a very personal twist to certain messages. Of course no one can communicate electronically with the same expressiveness as they can in person by means of facial expressions and body language; but they can have a good try, by using devices known as 'Smileys'.

A 'Smiley' is a simple code, an arrangement of three items of punctuation to make a face. The basic 'Smiley' consists of a colon, a dash and a closing bracket. The arrangement :-) looks like a sideways smiling face, and on many computers will convert automatically to ☺. This can be inserted at any point to indicate that you don't wish what you have said to be taken seriously. Similarly, a colon, dash and opening bracket :-(will convert on many computers to ☹, indicating disappointment. Less often used is the combination of semicolon, dash, then closing bracket ;-). This makes a winking face, indicating that something has been left unsaid.

How not to do it

The way people use e-mail provides a revealing insight into the way their company works, the way they and their colleagues think. Receptive people who are open to new ideas will tend to embrace the e-mail culture willingly, sending crisp, clear messages, whereas those who are un-adventurous and uncreative, who like to sound important while giving away as little as possible, will find it hard to break the habit.

Here is an example of how not to use e-mail, a management consultant attempting to explain the task he and his colleagues had performed for a particular client:

> *In the last engagement our charter was to help the executive team evolve the strategy to fit into the new environment and simultaneously to evolve the new environment to fit into the strategy.*

It sounds mind-boggling, doesn't it? And it means absolutely nothing. Dishing up pretentious nonsense to a client is one thing – many business people do it up to a point, and maybe management consultants do it more than most. But when someone writes this kind of rubbish to a *colleague*, can he really know what he is doing?

The excesses of management-speak are exposed most clearly in e-mail, which demands none of the starchy formality that is so familiar in letters written on headed company notepaper. Instead, it demands speed, crispness, quick-wittedness and accuracy. In e-mail more than in any other writing medium, your thought processes are revealed for all to see.

6. *Faxes and Memos*

Faxes

The great advantage of the facsimile message – now known everywhere by its three-letter abbreviation – is speed. Even e-mail is not in the same class. Whereas it can take several hours for an e-mail message to make its way via an electronic mailbox to its destination, a fax arrives instantly. You can be having a conversation with someone on the telephone while faxing them a document; a few seconds later, when the fax has passed through your machine and issued almost simultaneously from a machine at the other end, you can be discussing the content of that document.

When it comes to writing a fax, you may well have very little to do. The message – quotation, report, letter, memo, press cutting or whatever – may already be available, and it is simply a matter of conveying it to the intended reader as quickly as possible. Alternatively, you may be writing an original message with the intention of sending it by fax – in which case, there are a few more factors to consider.

Whatever the circumstances, there are a few steps that you should take before sending any fax:

- Give your own name, address, phone and fax number at the top of the first sheet, and, if you want to be doubly sure, at the top of every subsequent sheet. On the top sheet you must also state how many pages you are sending. This is vital in case the paper runs out or there is some other hitch at the receiving end – then the recipient can call you to clarify things

- Give the name, position in the organisation (if relevant) and fax number of the person to whom you are sending the message

- State the subject of the message, and whether it is urgent. This can make all the difference. Your reader may have a constant stream of messages arriving on his or her desk, but if they can see at a glance that yours concerns the issue of the moment (eg 'PROJECT X – LATEST NEWS'), then it will be read first

- Number each page

- Finally, if it is an important message, it is always best to telephone first and check that the receiver is ready for it. Much more essential, however, is to phone immediately afterwards to make sure that it has been received by the right person

Ideally, you should create a standard fax cover sheet, similar to your own distinctive letterhead, which will ensure you take care of many of these details. Here is a fax heading that is available with standard Windows 95 software:

Fax

To:	From:	
Company:	Pages:	(including this cover sheet)
Fax:	Date:	

Now you can get straight into your message. Because a fax is designed for immediacy rather than formality, you don't even have to write complete sentences. A short fax message, for instance, could start something like this:

Reaction to your proposal. Roger said No – too costly. Jane liked it, but thought it should be tested first …

Differences of style apart, you should write fax messages in much the same way as you would write a letter. Having given your name and the name of the recipient at the top, you don't need to start with 'Dear…', nor do you need to sign your name at the end. But if you feel these things give your message an appropriately personal touch, go ahead.

A fax is a versatile instrument. If you're in a real hurry there is no reason why you shouldn't handwrite several pages – as long as your handwriting is legible. More likely, you will type most messages, and occasionally handwrite a note at the end.

Certain business messages are particularly suited to sending by fax. An estimate or quotation is one. Although these can be sensitive documents, which might appear to demand confidentiality, many people want these details as quickly as possible, and prefer you to fax them.

A quotation sent by fax can be a mixture of formality and informality. Here is a textile conservator writing to a client:

To:	Abdul Khalidi	From:	Sarah Holtgrieve
Company:	Turkomania	Pages:	2 (including this cover sheet)
Fax:	001 22 333 4444	Date:	15 May 1998

Here is the quotation you requested for the Tulip textile. My embroiderer and I have worked on it to assess the time it will take to do the work. This is a major job on which I will have to bear substantial labour and material costs – so I must ask you for acceptance in writing, and a third of the payment in advance.

I hope the fair went well.

Detailed quotation follows on next sheet.

Page 2:
Sarah Holtgrieve
220 Ridgmount Gardens, London W11 7BC
Tel: 44 171 000 0000; Fax: 44 171 000 0000

15 May 1998

Abdul Khalidi
Turkomania
100 Anatolia Street
ISTANBUL
Turkey

ESTIMATE

To Conserve Ottoman Embroidery

<u>Embroidery with Tulip Pattern</u>

Patch the holes with suitable linen fabric. Conserve the existing embroidery. Line with linen and attach velcro strip.

Materials	£1,000
Labour	£2,000
VAT	£525
TOTAL	£3,525

VAT No: xxxx xxxxx

Terms

Acceptance in writing. First £1,000 payable in advance. Insured at owner's risk. Payment of remaining £2,525 immediately on completion of job.

The fax is especially useful for conveying rough images – maps, designs etc – that can then be discussed over the telephone before finalised designs are prepared and sent out.

There is one other important thing to remember about faxes: whereas a letter is sent in an envelope addressed to a single person, a fax issuing from a machine may be read by whoever happens to be walking past. Even if you are sending a fax to someone's home, or an office in which they work alone, things can go wrong – overenthusiastic cleaners, wandering colleagues, temperamental fax machines...

All these imponderables make it worth repeating the advice: *telephone immediately after sending* and make sure everything is in order.

Exercise: You have been asked to investigate the possibility of hiring a conference centre for a series of seminars. The requirement is for a room that will take 20 people, with movable tables and chairs, an overhead projector, flip chart and Powerpoint projector and screen. Lunch and tea/coffee breaks will also have to be organised. You have checked out Hargrave House, just outside Northampton, and reckon it will do nicely. Write a one-page fax, giving details of all facilities, necessary measurements, prices etc.

Then compose directions by road to Hargrave House. (Just think of some reasonably secluded place you know and try to translate your own route into detailed directions, with suitable-sounding landmarks.)

Compare your efforts with the Model Faxes in Chapter 16.

Memos

There are two types of memorandum – the confidential person-to-person memo, and the memo for wider circulation, or for the office noticeboard.

Personal memos are appropriate for all internal communications between members of an organisation. You may even have access to reusable memo envelopes. So if you have a suggestion, a point of view, a brief report or other story to tell and you don't want it forgotten, put it in a memo – and don't forget to keep a copy. If someone has your request/idea in writing, they have much less excuse for not acting on it. You can handwrite this kind of memo if you like, as long as your writing is perfectly legible, but if the message is more than a few lines long, it's much safer to type.

If you want a pay rise, for instance, it may be almost impossible to find an appropriate moment to corner your busy boss, or you may just feel embarrassed to ask for one in person. Besides, it is often easier to make a clear case in writing. If you do write a memo asking for a pay rise or have a similar demand, treat it very much like a letter of complaint: stick to the facts, and keep any pleading to an absolute minimum. No one likes to feel they are the victim of moral blackmail, but few will not respond positively to a well-argued case. Here is an example:

MEMORANDUM

Date: **10th March 1998**

From: **Philip Jones**

To: **Ron Wagstaffe**

Re: **Possible pay rise**

Dear Ron

Like everyone else, I was delighted to hear of the dramatic increase in the company's sales last month. It seems a good moment to write to you on my own behalf.

When I took this job nearly 12 months ago, it was on the basis that if I did my job well, and sales increased, I would be rewarded accordingly. I have not yet had any pay rise, and I hope you will agree that on any objective assessment, I am now entitled to one.

I look forward to hearing from you.

Yours

Phil

A memo like this is direct, polite and to the point, and should have a reasonable chance of success. But if you have raised the subject before and been given evasive answers, you may feel you need to put some pressure on.

In such circumstances, you might insert a paragraph like this:

> **As you may know, I stay in touch with several friends at my old company, and I learned the other day that the person who replaced me as marketing manager had just had an eight per cent pay rise – and I know that their sales increases have not matched ours. I am enjoying my work here more than ever and the last thing I want to do is look elsewhere, but I owe it to myself and my family to ensure that I am paid what I am worth. I hope you will give this matter your urgent attention.**

There is, of course, an implied threat in this paragraph, but it is based on fact, and it is accompanied by positive remarks about the employer, so it should not be taken amiss.

Writing a memo is no different from writing a letter, and all the same considerations of reader-awareness apply. A memo is just as much 'on the record' as a letter. The only significant difference is to do with etiquette. For example, a company taking on an employee will normally send a formal letter of appointment to the person's home, rather than merely sending them a memo on their first day. In the same way, any important change in someone's condition of employment should normally be communicated by letter, on headed notepaper. It doesn't matter so much with a pay rise, but courtesy dictates that any disciplinary matters, or notice of dismissal or redundancy, should be dealt with formally, by letter.

Organisational or information matters, however, are eminently suited to being dealt with by memo. The following circular memo could either be circulated – on paper or via e-mail – or posted on the noticeboard, depending on circumstances in your office:

This office will be closed for 12 days over Christmas, from 8pm on Wednesday 23 December until 8am on Monday, 4 January. If you need to make urgent contact with one of the directors during this period, Susan Wheeler will be available on 01305 000000 from 23–29 Dec, and Richard Mills will be available on 01273 111111 from 30 Dec to 3 Jan. If you need to gain access to the building, please contact Simon, John or Dave on 0171 379 0000 and arrange to pick the keys up from them.

Memos like this are sent to make sure that everyone gets the message. If you merely speak to the people who are present at that particular moment, you run the risk that someone who was away, or on holiday that particular day, will come back and be unaware of your announcement.

The one important thing to remember with circular memos is to be clear – clear about who they are for, clear about what the message is, clear about who is affected and clear about the person to whom anyone should report on this particular issue.

The following memo, for instance, leaves a lot to desired:

Everyone, please note. Don't go home without submitting a copy of any sales transaction.

Bill Forrest, Sales and Marketing Director

All sorts of questions might arise for the reader: Does he really mean everyone? But I don't normally deal with sales. Anyway, where should I submit a record of such a transaction? Does he really want them all piling up on his desk? And if I pop home for lunch, have I got to do it then?

This would be much better:

To: All sales staff

From: Bill Forrest

Re: Notification of sales

Please make sure that you inform me of any sales by the end of the working day. Just put a copy of the sale document in Julia's in-tray.

Exercise: You and a colleague have volunteered to organise the staff Christmas party, for which your own management is prepared to make a contribution. Having checked out a local wine bar and talked to the manager, you think you've found the ideal place. Write a memo for the office noticeboard (which can also be sent to everyone by e-mail, or by post to others outside your head office) explaining what's on offer, cost per head etc. Ask people to confirm whether they want to come, and whether they want to bring a guest or guests.

Or: Imagine yourself as the head of corporate communications in a publicly quoted company. You have just endured several exasperating months putting together the company's annual report, attempting to reconcile the conflicting views of various directors. The project has left you precious little time to attend to your normal duties, not to mention having damaged your relations with at least one department. Write a one-page memo to the managing director explaining why you want to hire an external writer to do the annual report next year.

Model Memos for both scenarios are given in Chapter 16.

The Right Style

7. The Importance of Grammar

NOW THAT you know what you want to say, you are more than halfway there. You are like a potter who has mixed his materials and given a basic shape to the chosen article. But without a glaze, the article is unfinished, not suitable for commercial use.

In the next part of this book, we aim to smooth off the rough edges, and put a glaze on your writing, so that it is ready to be used in any business context. We begin with grammar and punctuation. Then we come to some of the common pitfalls of business writing – wasted words, jargon or management-speak, and vagueness. Finally, we consider some of the minutiae of style, and those troublesome phrases and expressions that can let down even experienced, fluent writers.

Grammar, that stuff we learned – or didn't learn – at school . . . Isn't it terribly complicated? Will I ever remember it all?

Don't worry about it. Grammar is largely a matter of putting the words in the right order. It is a means to an end. Meaning is what really matters, and if the meaning is clear, you can be almost certain that the grammar is okay. Some of the finer points are dealt with in later chapters (in case you are not sure about the meaning of nouns, pronouns, prepositions and so on).

The surest way of being grammatically correct is to keep your writing simple, so that's what we're going to try to do here.

The right order

Many problems of grammar and construction are caused by simple sloppiness. Sloppy writers often try to get too much off their chest at once. They will start a sentence, then add extraneous thoughts to it, or they start in the wrong place and take ages to get to the point. By not pausing to think about how to sructure their thoughts and ideas, they write sentences so convoluted that the poor reader gets to the end of the document without knowing what it's all about; they then have to read it again, in an irritated frame of mind, or they switch off completely.

We all write thoughtlessly at times. But in business, we can't afford to lose readers in this way. So we must *always* read everything through from the reader's point of view. Is it clear? Or is it ambiguous? Will the reader grasp the point as quickly as possible? Is the reader getting the right message? Have I started in the right place?

Listing

Everybody loves lists. We make shopping lists, lists of daily tasks to do, lists of people to invite to a party, lists of favourite film stars or imaginary football teams. One of the reasons these lists are satisfying is that they are lists of the same things – lettuce, eggs, milk etc – and are easy to follow.

Lists are a vital feature of business writing, but people get into trouble when they try to make lists of things that are not really alike. Here's an example of a list within a sentence, from an internal bank memorandum:

> *The brochure will contain an application form lasered with: customer's name, address, account number, National Insurance number and to include interest rates.*

The reader gets to the end, and immediately has to read the sentence again. One moment the writer was listing customer

details; then he switched to interest rates – simply because he had forgotten to put them in the right place.

That sentence should have read:

> **The brochure will give details of current interest rates, and will contain an application form lasered with the customer's name, address, account number and National Insurance number.**

Now it makes sense; we've got the interest rates out of the way, and gone on to list the customer's personal details that are lasered on the application form: name, address, account number and National Insurance number.

Let's look at a list in the form of bullet points:

We have

- **introduced a new management structure**
- **assessed the scope for further acquisitions**
- **started to decentralise responsibilities**

That's nice and clear, isn't it? It is a list of actions taken. But in its original form, it read as follows:

Much has been achieved already:

- *the introduction of a new management structure*
- *assessing the scope for further acquisitions*
- *the first steps have been taken to decentralise responsibilities*

This is hopelessly confusing; the writer has not bothered to compile or phrase the list properly, and we move from a noun in the first instance to an entire sentence as the third and final item. The revised version, by beginning each point with a verb, provides clarity and consistency.

Sentence structure

The solution to the problem of sentence structure is the same as with listing: start in the right place, and keep it simple.

Here are some paragraphs from corporate literature that can easily be rearranged so that they start in the right place and read more clearly:

ORIGINAL:
Could you please bring with you to the interview the attached forms duly completed.

IMPROVED:
Please complete the attached forms and bring them with you.

Why is the second version so much clearer and easier to read? Because, in the original version, the writer has thought and written only from his own point of view: 'What do I want? I want them to bring the forms with them – and of course, they'll have to complete the forms first.' In the second version, the writer has paused to think from the reader's point of view: What should they do? They should complete the forms and bring them with them.'

On the whole, the simplest constructions are best. Who does what to whom? Subject, verb, object – no possible confusion. If in doubt, you may well need to change the subject of the sentence, or introduce a pronoun – 'you' or 'we', for instance.

Take another example:

ORIGINAL:
We are not clearly recognised as an Insurance Broker, often being confused with an Insurance Company by customers.

In this instance, the writer has again begun, naturally enough, to write from the company's point of view ('We…'), only to discover by the end of the sentence that what he is really talking about is the customers' viewpoint. The result is a clumsy, ill-ordered sentence. The solution is simple: make 'Customers' the subject:

IMPROVED:
Customers do not clearly recognise us as insurance brokers; many of them think we are an insurance company.

Changing the subject – and consequently the order of the sentence – is often a good way out of this sort of confusion. Here's a more complicated example:

ORIGINAL:

The comments received (and there have been a good number) on the new design and size of the annual report have been most complimentary in that it was easy to read and find one's way around the various concepts of our business and in terms of industry information.

This is a very unwieldy sentence. The first problem arises from the use of an abstract noun ('comments') as the subject. What comments by whom and about what? It's going to take a lot of explaining. The second half of the sentence loses its way because the writer has lazily written 'in that...' before shoving in everything else he could think of. And what is 'in terms of industry information' doing at the end?

There's far too much material here for one sentence. It needs to be cut into at least two sentences. And the points must be arranged more logically. How about this?

IMPROVED:

We have received many compliments on the new annual report. People like the size, the design, the amount of industry information, and the way it guides the reader round the various parts of our business.

This is intelligible and logically ordered. Again, the right subject for each sentence is crucial: 'We' in the first sentence, 'People' in the second.

Subject–verb agreement

Here is another pitfall for the sloppy writer. It's no good choosing the right subject if you then forget about it and insert a verb that doesn't agree with it. All you need is care and precision. If the subject is singular, so is the verb:

A tree [*singular subject – one tree*] grows [*singular verb*].

Likewise if the subject is plural:

Trees [*plural subject – at least two trees*] grow [*plural verb*].

All very obvious – but when other words get in the way, people often become confused. The following sentence appeared in some internal literature in a bank:

Credits, on the other hand, which includes…

That's a plural noun ('credits') with a singular verb ('includes'). They don't agree. The sentence should read:

Credits [*plural*], on the other hand, which include [*plural*]…

Sometimes it is easy to forget which word is the subject. You might write: 'A portion of the revenues are subject to tax.' This is wrong; it is not the revenues that are subject to tax, but only a portion – one (singular) portion. You should write:

A portion of the revenues is subject to tax.

The same should be true of percentages, and all collective nouns: a crowd gathers (a lot of people, but only one crowd); government governs; management decides; XYZ Ltd aims to satisfy its customers.

The last example is important; a company is always a single legal entity, and should take a singular verb for both legal and grammatical reasons. The fact is, however, that most people think of companies and organisations as plural – and a lot of people write that way too, eg 'The council are coming to fix my drains.' Not correct – it's only one council, isn't it? But it would be correct to say: The men from the council are coming to fix my drains' because now you have a plural subject, 'men'.

The temptation to use a plural verb with a collective noun is a strong one, not least because you don't want to sound impersonal when writing about your company or organisation. The simple answer to the problem is to be correct on those occasions when you need to speak for the organisation: 'XYZ Rail has a customer charter...' But as soon as you can, just introduce the word 'we' – 'At XYZ Rail, we try to keep our customers informed...' From then on, 'we' can become the subject, taking a plural verb.

For he/she confusion, see Chapter 12.

Pronouns

A pronoun is a word that stands in for a noun. Most pronouns have a different form depending on whether they are the subject or object in a sentence. So if we write a paragraph or two about Emily Smith, the subject will soon become 'she'; if 'she' is the object, we will refer to 'her'.

These are the essential pronouns:

Subject	Object
I	me
you	you
he, she, it	him, her, it
we	us
they	them

A common illiteracy, more often spoken than written, is to use the object form when it should be the subject. For instance: 'My mate and me went to the pub.'

It should, of course, be 'My mate and I went to the pub.' We are both, after all, the subject of this particular sentence (the pub being the object).

Or we sometimes hear people say things like: 'A policeman told my wife and I we couldn't park there.'

This should be 'my wife and me', because the policeman is the subject and we are the object of the sentence.

In examples like this, the correct form is easily arrived at by removing the other person from the sentence, and checking which pronoun is right. It would be uncommonly perverse to write 'Me went to the pub' or 'A policeman told I...'

Less obviously wrong is the following example: 'It was him who wrote the letter.'

In this instance, the writer has been confused by the introductory 'It was ...' and assumed that because 'it' is the subject of the sentence, 'him' must be the object. This is not the case. Who wrote the letter? *He* did. 'He' is the subject of the sentence – even if he is introduced by another subject, 'It'. The object, of course, is 'letter.'

The correct version, therefore, is: 'It was he who wrote the letter.'

Here's an even less obvious error: 'I hated him smoking in the office.'

Actually, it wasn't 'him' I hated, but his smoking. The sentence should read: 'I hated his smoking in the office.'

The other common mistake made with pronouns is when the suffix -self or -selves is added unnecessarily. There are only two occasions when you should use this form:

1. Intensively, as in 'I did it myself' (meaning I had no help)

2. Reflexively, as in 'He included himself in the working group'

The intensive or reflexive form can only be used with the ordinary pronoun. It has no place in sentences like these:

Please return this form to myself. (It should be **Please return this form to me.**)

If this is convenient to yourself ... (It should be **If this is convenient for you ...**)

Do you remember the hotel letter in Chapter 1? In its original form, this referred to 'the bar docket signed by yourself'. But I usually sign things by myself, even when I've been in a bar all evening... The writer should simply have written 'the bar docket you signed...'

Tenses

Just as switching between singular and plural can be confusing, so can switches in tenses. If you begin a sentence in the past tense, you should stay there. The main verb must decide – that is, the verb on which the rest of the sentence depends. In each of the examples given below, the main verb is <u>underlined</u>:

I <u>said</u> I was willing to come.

NOT

I <u>said</u> I am willing to come.

'I said I was willing to come.' That was what I said then. Things might be different now. I might have another engagement. If the main verb is in the past tense, the subsidiary verb can't be in the present. And it certainly can't be in the future:

You <u>wrote</u> (past tense) to us on February 11 to say that you will (future tense) be closing your account.

This is much too big a jump. The following sentence is correct:

You wrote (past) to us on February 11th to say that you would (conditional) be closing your account.

Using the word 'would' means the second half of the sentence is conditional on the first. Well, the customer might have said that then, but is it still the case now? Maybe not.

You could always write:

I <u>understand</u> from your letter of February 11 that you will be closing your account.

This is fine. 'I understand' brings the situation into the present. 'As things stand, you *will* be closing your account.' The reader can make the jump from present to future.

If you want to move from the past into the present in one sentence, there is a way. You use the present perfect tense ('I have done'; 'I have been'). This is subtly different from the simple past tense ('I did'; 'I was'). In both cases, the event is clearly in the past, but in the present perfect tense you are placing a past event in a present context. When you say 'you have done' something, it seems closer in time than 'I did something'.

The following sentence is an uneasy mixture of the two:

I <u>was</u> sorry to hear that you have not made use of your Air Miles points.

It should be either:

I <u>was</u> sorry to hear that you had not made use of your Air Miles points. (Everything in the past tense)

OR

I <u>am</u> sorry to hear that you have not made use of your Air Miles points. (Past events brought into a present context)

Like most grammar, it's simply a matter of putting everything in the right order, and trying to make it easy for the reader.

Modifiers

A modifier is any part of a sentence that comes outside the main subject-verb-object section, modifying or explaining its significance. In the following sentences, the modifier is underlined, and subject, verb and object are signified by (s), (v) or (o) immediately after the relevant word:

<u>Whenever it rains</u>, we [s] use [v] umbrellas [o].

The chief executive [s], <u>who doesn't suffer fools gladly</u>, chased [v] the interviewer [o] out of his office.

In the first instance, the modifier could just as well be put at the end: 'We (s) use (v) umbrellas (o) whenever it rains. But in the second instance, it would obviously change the meaning radically if we wrote: 'The chief executive (s) chased (v) the interviewer (o), who doesn't suffer fools gladly, out of the office.' Now the modifier clearly applies to the object, the interviewer.

Modifiers are commonly misused by being put in the wrong place. Let's take a look at an example:

Having taken a two-hour lunch break, my boss gave me a severe reprimand.

Taken literally, this suggests it was the boss who took a two-hour lunch break. It needs to be rearranged:

My boss reprimanded me for taking a two-hour lunch break.

Or there's the old favourite: 'I met a man with a wooden leg called Fred' to which the traditional response is: 'What's his other leg called?' A clearer sentence would be: 'I met a man called Fred, who had a wooden leg.'

Here are some less startling, but equally avoidable, examples of misused modifiers, the first taken from bank correspondence:

Having raised the interest rates on our Diamond Reserve account, they were then greater than those we were paying on our Crown Reserve account.

This is a confusing sentence to read, because the introductory phrase requires the subject to be 'we', the bank. 'Having raised the interest rates..., we found that they were higher...' would be fine. Or, if you want 'interest rates' to be the subject of the sentence, you should turn it round: 'The interest rates...have been raised, and are now higher than ...'

Here's another one, from a credit card marketing material:

As an established XYZ holder, this loan gives you fast access to any amount up to £10,000.

Again, the reader – this time the established XYZ card holder – is led to believe by the modifier that he or she will be the subject of the main sentence. It would be fine if it said: 'As an established XYZ card holder, you can enjoy fast access... through this loan.' As it is, it is ungrammatical. More important, it just doesn't flow – the reader has to work too hard to follow it.

Here's an example from a magazine which conjures up an intriguing picture:

> *Apart from water, camels are the most valuable possession of the Bedouin. These days they wear trainers under their traditional Arab robes, get their food in tins from supermarkets, and play Gameboys and guitars, yet they cling tenaciously to simple values like their sense of community in which everything, including problems, are shared.*

Finally, here's a classic misused modifier from a local newspaper report:

> *When Her Majesty had broken the traditional bottle of champagne over the bows of the ship, she slid slowly and gracefully down the slipway, entering the water with scarcely a splash.*

The lesson is simple. Keep the subject of the sentence, whether implied or stated, constantly in mind, and be consistent. And for heaven's sake, read it through! Even professional writers make mistakes.

8. *Punctuation*

PUNCTUATION is one of the most effective weapons in the writer's armoury. It has a simple purpose: to help the reader to pause in the right places. Once you know the function of each form of punctuation, you should be able to punctuate effectively just by looking at every sentence from the reader's point of view. From this point on, common sense will matter far more than rules.

Now let's consider the tools at our disposal.

Apostrophe

An apostrophe has two main uses:

1. To indicate possession by replacing the word 'of'. Thus, we refer to *the company's Fleet Street branch* instead of *the Fleet Street branch of the company*; *Jeffrey Archer's novels*; *the customer's expectations* (or *customers' expectations*, if you are thinking of a number of customers).

   The possessive pronouns – *his, hers, its, theirs, yours, ours* – do not require an apostrophe.

   Now and then, you may not be sure where to put the apostrophe. Is it *the trainers' wives* or *the trainer's wives*? Is it *the girl's choir* or *the girls' choir*?

   If in doubt, you will always get the right answer if you put the 'of' back in. Ask yourself if you mean *the wives of the trainer*, or the *wives of the trainers*. Whatever the answer is, you put the apostrophe immediately afterwards. In this case, the answer is *trainers*. If you wrote *the trainer's wives*, you would be implying bigamy! In the same way, is it the *choir of the girl*, or the *choir of the girls*? Answer: *girls*. So put the apostrophe after *girls*.

But should it be *Mr Jones's house* or *Mr Jones' house*? When a word already ends with an 's', some people don't like putting an extra 's' after the apostrophe. The best test is what you would actually say. If you would say Mr Jones's house – as most people would – then write it.

Do not confuse possessive with plural. *Mr and Mrs Jones* are *the Joneses*, not t*he Jones's*. And their front door is *the Joneses' front door* (*the front door of the Joneses*, if you put the 'of' back in).

Apples and pears are simply plural, *apples and pears*, and not, as greengrocers have mistakenly called them for generations, *apple's and pear's*.

2. To indicate a missing letter or missing letters: 'It's' (meaning 'it is'); I'll (meaning 'I will'); 'the class of '88' (meaning '1988').

If, like all too many people, you confuse the possessive 'its' with 'it's', which is a contraction of 'it is', then remember this sentence: 'It's a good dog that knows its master.' In the first instance, an apostrophe replaces the missing letter. In the second, the possessive 'its' requires no apostrophe.

Brackets

Avoid brackets if possible; they break up the flow of your writing. If you can use dashes or commas, do. If you find yourself explaining something at length in brackets, perhaps you should have another look at what you are writing. Would it not be better to make the necessary explanation first, without brackets, then carry on with the next subject in a separate sentence?

The only time brackets are more or less essential is when providing brief technical explanations or acknowledging sources. For instance:

> **At the moment, we retain 76–80% of our graduate accounts (*Network Research* September 1995).**

Common sense should tell you where to put the full stop. If the information in brackets relates precisely to that sentence and that sentence only, then you should enclose it within the sentence, as above.

Occasionally, you might need to add an entire sentence in brackets. This extract from *The Economist* on the subject of America's cellular telephones provides examples of both kinds of brackets:

> **Until recently, most of America's cellular carriers faced only a single competitor in their region and generated vast cash flows. This cosy existence has been ruined by a combination of a telecoms act passed last year and a new generation of 'personal communications services' (PCS), cheap mobile phones that use new digital technology. PCS's roll-out has not been smooth and some carriers overbid for wireless licences at auctions held by the Federal Communications Commission (FCC), leaving several in or near bankruptcy. (Bidders are now being offered the chance to return some or all of the licences.) Nevertheless, cellular carriers are suddenly finding themselves with lots of new competitors – up to six in some metropolitan markets.**

Colon

A colon introduces things. Think of it as an arrow that directs the reader onwards. Use a colon whenever you are about to supply some kind of list, quotation or explanation. Just look back through this book and you will see plenty of colons used in this way. Normally, you would not have a capital letter after a colon, as you are not starting a new sentence:

> **Players should bring the following: tracksuit, training shoes, change of clothes, jacket and tie.**

With a more complicated list, set out as, say, a series of numbered points or bullet points, it may seem sensible to start each new point with a capital letter, particularly as some of the items listed may consist of more than one sentence. The beginning of Chapter 3 provides an example of a numbered list introduced in this way.

Comma

The comma simply invites the reader to take a short pause within a sentence. So use one whenever you want to separate one phrase, or item, from the next part of the sentence. For example: 'Under John Evans's direction, the company boosted its profits.'

Use commas when you want to insert something in parenthesis, such as a title: 'Gordon Brown, Chancellor of the Exchequer, said ... '

Or a qualifying phrase: 'There will be times, over the years of your student life, when money is tight.'

The basic sentences, in these two instances, are: 'Gordon Brown said...' and 'There will be times when money is tight.' The qualifying parts are within the commas, which are functioning like brackets without breaking the flow of the sentence.

The following sentence is more tricky: 'The proposal included the following sections: introduction, scope of the work, schedule, and cost.'

Do you need the last comma? Take it out and see. Now it could be read as three sections: 'introduction, scope of the work, schedule and cost.' If you mean it to have four sections, then include the final comma. And ignore people who tell you you should never put a comma before 'and'.

Don't forget that a comma is only a short pause. It is not enough to separate independent thoughts. Take this example:

Mailing was very complicated, many clients telephoned for clarification.

As it stands, a comma is not enough to separate what are basically two separate sentences on different subjects. You could make it one sentence by using a linking word like 'with':

> **Mailing was very complicated, with many clients telephoning for clarification.**

Or you could keep it as two sentences, and use appropriate punctuation to separate the two – a semi-colon or a full stop:

> **Mailing was very complicated; many clients telephoned for clarification.**

Some of the commonest errors of punctuation occur with 'however', 'therefore', 'nevertheless' etc. For further guidance, see Chapter 12.

Dash

The dash is a versatile form of punctuation that some people never use, and others use to excess. You can use a dash instead of a comma when you want a slightly longer pause, with a hint of drama. For instance:

> **Every effort the company made was in order to keep out one man – Robert Maxwell.**

A comma in this instance would not be enough. The sentence would lose its dramatic point. You could use a colon, but they are better at the start of a sentence.

The other common use for dashes is when you think of something that is relevant, but find it hard to include it in the sentence:

> **Banks and building societies have to pay VAT on the components of mailshots – forms, envelopes, and other stationery – but because they themselves are VAT-exempt, they can't claim the tax back.**

In such instances, the dashes are fulfilling the same purpose as brackets, but they are much easier on the eye and closer to the way we ourselves speak – in sentences punctuated with thoughts and ideas.

Full stop

Everyone knows that a full stop ends a sentence, but not everyone uses full stops when they should.

The following sentence is really two sentences, precariously held together with a lot of commas:

> *Unfortunately, once the correct details have been noted, the backdated premiums will need to be collected, therefore, the first debit will be for £176.07.*

A better version would be:

> **When we have noted the correct details, we will need to collect the backdated premiums. Your first payment of £176.07 will be due on …**

Short sentences are almost invariably clearer than long ones. So use more full stops. (Also see next chapter.)

Hyphen

The hyphen is sadly underused. It performs a valuable service by linking two words that might otherwise have equal weight in a sentence.

It is claimed that an American industrial company once lost $25,000 because a supervisor ordered 'six foot long rods'; he was sent six foot-long rods, instead of the six-foot-long rods he actually needed.

The key to deciding whether to hyphenate is the question: Do we have two words that belong together, perhaps forming a single adjective – or, more rarely, a single noun? If we do, we should hyphenate.

So, when we look at something 'in the long term', we don't hyphenate (long is the adjective, term is the noun – no possible confusion). When we take a 'long-term view', we do hyphenate, because two words ('long' and 'term') are being used as a single adjective ('long-term') qualifying the noun 'view'.

The following terms or phrases are made much clearer by the use of hyphens:

cost-effective programmes	reply-paid application forms
self-service cafeterias	commission-free travel
point-of-sale requirements	facilities
follow-up activity	in-house services
non-respondent customers	the account-holding branch
duty-free goods	adult-to-adult
post-college loan	communication
runner-up prizes	fixed-rate consumer loan

Other common adjectival phrases that should be hyphenated are: *take-away, face-to-face, price-sensitive, low-cost, high-volume.*

Inverted commas

Inverted commas are used primarily for quotations, and it is purely a matter of house style whether they are single or double. Reported speech in newspapers is usually in double inverted commas:

"This is a historic day," said the Prime Minister.

But in many books and magazines, as in this book, the style is to use single inverted commas for direct quotations.

Whichever prevailing style is chosen, the opposite is used for quotes-within-quotes:

'I will be there on Thursday,' said Samantha, 'provided my "minders" will let me go.'

The reader should never see something in inverted commas and not know why. In the last example, the context would make it clear that Samantha was using the term 'minders' ironically.

Inverted commas can also be used for titles, phrases or technical terms that need to be differentiated from the body of the text:

The term 'electronic commerce' is used to describe shopping, banking and all sorts of other transactions that can now be conducted via the Internet.

We use inverted commas in order to make the reader pause and change gear. So we shouldn't use them when we want the reader to gallop easily along. There is nothing more irritating than reading text that keeps interrupting itself with superfluous inverted commas:

When a bank lends money it does not gain any 'control' over the direction of a business.

Do the inverted commas really add anything in this instance? We can imagine why the writer has used them – because it is other people who imagine that banks have control, when in fact they don't. But the sentence would provide an equally clear and effective assertion without the inverted commas – and it would be easier to read.

Every time you put something in quotes you are distancing yourself from it. You are saying: 'These are not my words.' This can suggest lack of confidence or unwillingness to take responsibility, depending on the context. Diffident writers borrow other people's expressions and put them in quotation marks. If you want to give a dynamic, positive impression, use your own words.

Question mark

If a sentence is a question, it should end with a question mark, eg: Would you mind notifying us as soon as the sale is completed?

But if a sentence merely contains a reported question, it should not have a question mark, eg: I asked him if he would mind notifying us as soon as the sale was completed.

Semi-colon

The semi-colon does a completely different job from a colon. Whereas a colon introduces, a semi-colon separates. It signifies a pause that is longer and more meaningful than a comma, but not as emphatic as a full stop.

Some writers like semi-colons; others don't. If you don't like them, you can probably manage without. But most of us find them useful as a way of separating a series of linked thoughts or items. A semi-colon can be a good way of maintaining a reader's interest; it suggests that there's more to come on the same theme.

Here is one instance:

The guests included: Mr Tony Blair, Prime Minister; Mrs Margaret Beckett, President of the Board of Trade; Mr Gordon Brown, Chancellor of the Exchequer.

Exercise: Add punctuation to the following sentences, so that their meaning is clear:

1. This is how it works you insert the coin pull the lever then retrieve the goods

2. Sam never really wanted the job just the kudos

3. The role of business is to create wealth and not whatever people say to create jobs

4. John Biggins one of our salesmen will call on you on Monday

5. Never forget its a good dog that knows its master

6. A week of freezing temperatures −15C on average caused the lake to freeze over which brought out the skaters in their day glo outfits

7. Its amazing said Joan when I showed her the new design

Solutions

1. This is how it works: you insert the coin, pull the lever, then retrieve the goods.

2. Sam never really wanted the job, just the kudos.

3. The role of business is to create wealth, and not, whatever people say, to create jobs.

4. John Biggins, one of our salesmen, will call on you on Monday.

5. Never forget: it's a good dog that knows its master.

6. A week of freezing temperatures (-15C on average) caused the lake to freeze over – which brought out the skaters in their day-glo outfits.

7. 'It's amazing,' said Joan, when I showed her the new design.

9. *Plain English (without waffle)*

WHEN WE WRITE in a corporate role to sound authoritative and yet simultaneously friendly and obliging, we often use unnecessary words, and end up sounding imprecise and unprofessional. A typical example is this sign-off sentence: 'I will make contact in the next few days to arrange a mutually convenient time to have a meeting.' This is so ultra-obliging as to be absurd. As if you would arrange an 'inconvenient' time! All you need is: 'I will be in touch soon to arrange a meeting.'

Or here's a management training company introducing one of its programmes:

> *The information that follows will provide you with an in-depth look at its process and content.*

What is the purpose of this sentence? It is to persuade the reader to read on for further details. It could simply say: 'This is how it works.' But the writer is so wrapped up in management-speak that he feels obliged to offer an 'in-depth look' at 'process and content'. If only he could hear the reader thinking: 'Get on with it!'

A recent study of company reports showed that when company chairmen used long-winded expressions and evasive language, their companies were usually in trouble. By contrast, successful companies were more inclined to use short, punchy and factual words and sentences, sending out clear messages.

Defensive writing

Verbal diarrhoea affects people in many different ways, but most of it springs from a desire to sound important, to impress and reassure while protecting the writer in his or her job. People flannel because they are on the defensive. I was provided with a classic example a few years ago when I wrote to my bank to highlight the poor quality of some of the bank's writing; since I teach effective writing, I accompanied my complaint with an offer of help. I also enclosed an example of a misleading 'Notice to Customers'.

The response I received came from the 'Head of Development and Training Operations' – a title which carried its own warning of impending verbosity. The second paragraph is worth quoting in full:

> *At this moment in time, the Bank continues to invest heavily in training and development initiatives that contribute to the advancement of our challenging business objectives. The development of employee potential is a major focus of these programmes. Our Leadership & Management Competence Training addresses a very wide range of personal management and leadership skills development.*

In essence, all this paragraph really means is: 'The bank already runs training courses for its staff.' But instead of a single sentence with a single verb and two or three nouns, the writer wastes his time and mine employing between 20 and 25 nouns, depending on whether you count nouns used adjectivally. Why should I care about his 'challenging business objectives', whatever they might be? And what are training programmes about, if not 'the development of employee potential'?

The letter goes on for five paragraphs, referring to a 'comprehensive training infrastructure' supporting 'the diverse and changing needs of the business' and explaining that 'the immediate need for an external supplier is limited'. But, he adds: 'In the event that our business needs require the contracting of an external supplier, we will certainly consider your company.'

The letter looks superficially like a courteous and detailed response. In fact, it is nothing of the sort. What should have been the purpose of this letter? First, it needed to respond to a customer's complaint, which it completely failed to do. There was no mention of the misleading 'Notice to Customers', which remained unchanged for several months.

Secondly, it was supposed to get rid of me, which it could have accomplished quite easily and politely in two sentences. If the bank is already running training courses on effective writing, what could be more reasonable than to thank me for my interest and put me 'on file' for the foreseeable future?

Instead, the Head of Development and Training Operations tried to suffocate my complaint in an avalanche of words. The point is not whether or not this kind of verbiage is to your taste: the point is that it does not do the job. He wanted to give me the brush-off, and he failed. This letter remains, to my mind, a classic example of superficially polite words actually being used as bricks to build a wall between writer and reader.

Tautology and other crimes

There is a prime example of tautology – using different words to say something twice – in the letter quoted above. The fourth paragraph reads: 'In the event that our business needs require the contracting of an external supplier...' You can have needs, or you can require things, but you can't have 'needs requiring'. The whole sentence is absurdly convoluted anyway. Why not just say 'If we need to use an external supplier...'?

Here is another example of corporate flannel, which happens to contain two common examples of tautology:

> *We have analysed our past history of our commercial dealings with your respectable company... We are more interested to*

learn about the future prospects, which we may have, and the reasons as to why we have not realised any business since that time.'

History, like experience, is always past. And prospects, like plans, are bound to be for the future. So let's get rid of all the wasted words from that paragraph:

We have analysed our previous dealings with your company, and we are keen to find out why we have not done any business since then.

Exercise: It's easy enough, once you work out what you are really trying to say, to cut out waffle. Why not try it with these few sentences and paragraphs, all taken from recent business correspondence:

1. The most significant accounting issue we encountered was the policy for depreciation and obsolescence provisions. Our work showed that there was an excess of provision which could be released back to our profit.

2. In the latest results of our ongoing customer service research, it's very encouraging to see how customers' satisfaction with our overall service level has shown an increase over the last few periods.

3. I hope this answers your query in full. Please do not hesitate to contact me with any further queries on the above or on any other matter.

4. I would firstly like to assure you that the safety of all the products we sell is of paramount importance and we would not knowingly sell any item that we felt was liable to cause injury.

Preferred versions:

1. We discovered that too much money was being set aside for depreciation and obsolescence.

2. The latest research is encouraging: it shows that customers are increasingly satisfied with our service.

3. If you have any queries, please get in touch.

4. We give absolute priority to safety, and would never knowingly sell any item that might cause injury.

In the above exercise, we can identify some of the commonest ways of waffling. There is often a temptation to add abstract nouns, so that instead of improving 'service', we improve 'service levels'. Rather than deal with 'customers', managers love to talk about their 'customer base'. These abstract nouns may make management sound more like a science, and may make managers feel more important, but they take the reader further away from reality – and ultimately make it more difficult for organisations to tackle people and issues in a direct and dynamic way.

If you want to get rid of wasted words, avoid the following:

- Tautology: 'future plans'; 'past experience'

- Stilted language: 'prior to'; 'commencement'; 'in respect of'; 'with regard to'; 'on ... basis' (why say 'on a monthly basis' when you can simply say 'every month'?)

- Abstract nouns: 'situation'; 'provision'; 'environment'; 'programme'; 'level'; 'process'. Examples: 'business environment' (why say 'in this business environment', when you mean 'in this business'?); 'programme of meetings'; 'co-operation level'; 'rationalisation process'

- Unnecessarily emphatic adjectives: 'real'; 'key'; 'current'; adverbs: 'very'; 'extremely'; 'really'; 'basically'; 'honestly'; 'sincerely'

Why use several words when one will do? And why use long words when you can use short ones? Save your printer ink, and do your reader a favour.

Common examples:

Wasted words	**Preferred phrases**
at this moment in time	**now**
at an early date / in the near future	**soon**
accommodation	**home/house**
it came to light	**we found**
a wide range of	**many**
due to the fact that	**because**
it is our understanding that	**we understand**
we are of the opinion that	**we believe**
this affords us the opportunity	**this allows us**
in the event that	**if**
I am not in a position to	**I cannot**
in view of the fact that	**since**
with regard to	**about**
along the lines of	**like**
with the result that	**so that**
is in our possession	**we have**
few and far between	**few**

Shorter is almost always better. But you need variety, too. If you use the same words over and over again, you may start to sound monotonous. The best test is to read it to yourself. If it sounds better, then *just occasionally* use two or three words when one would probably do.

Officious, starchy language is just as bad. It creates a barrier between writer and reader. Just consider the following examples, from a leading clearing bank, writing to a customer:

> *If for any reason you are unable to provide immediate funds to adjust the position...*

PLAIN ENGLISH
If you cannot pay any money in...

Or this:

> *I cannot trace any agreement between us for overdraft facilities*

and I shall be grateful, therefore, if you will arrange for an immediate remittance...

PLAIN ENGLISH
You have no overdraft arrangement with us, so please pay in no less than ...

The same starchiness can be found in an internal memo:

May I take this opportunity to offer my compliments to all concerned.

PLAIN ENGLISH
Well done, everyone!

In each of these examples, the use of everyday, conversational English touches the reader far more powerfully. More important, it does the job better.

Nounitis

Now let's look at some more detailed examples of jargon, or management-speak. You will usually notice a proliferation of nouns – underlined in the following example, with verbs in bold:

*The key to the success of the new training programme **was** the utilisation of customer feedback to **change** the existing training process to better **meet** customer needs. (seven nouns, three verbs)*

This sort of pompous management-speak is meant to sound as if something incredibly sophisticated is going on, when it's all really quite straightforward. The writer is trying to sound important: he's got a dose of nounitis. The answer: a quick injection of verbs:

*The new training programme **worked** because we **asked** customers what they **thought**, and **made** appropriate changes. (three nouns, four verbs)*

Here's another one:

> *Customer <u>feedback</u> was* **solicited** *to* **determine** *satisfaction <u>levels</u> and <u>areas</u> for <u>improvement.</u> This <u>feedback</u> was* **obtained** *through <u>surveys</u> and group <u>meetings</u>.*

Another severe dose of nounitis. Again, no fewer than seven nouns (I'm not counting the words 'customer', 'satisfaction' and 'group', which are all being used as adjectives), and only three verbs – making two dreadfully turgid sentences. The solution: wipe away three of those nouns, inject a verb, and we might even be able to tell the story in a single sentence:

> *We* **held** *<u>surveys</u> and group <u>meetings</u> with our <u>customers</u> to* **find** *out where they* **felt** *<u>improvements</u> could be* **made.**

It looks easy, doesn't it? And it is certainly achievable. Most of us try to justify ourselves when we write, and that does not help us communicate. It tends to make us think and write defensively. Writing plain English takes effort. But you can do it. If you suffer from nounitis, one thing you can do is check your writing and try to use a verb for every noun.

Just think. Remember your reader. Avoid abstract nouns. Use verbs. Say who is doing what to whom. And test for sound: read it back to yourself – aloud if you like – and see if it sounds natural. Is it the kind of thing you would say if the reader were in the same room? If it is, then it should do the job.

Exercise: Now try putting some of these stilted, jargon-riddled sentences into plain English:

1. I have concerns regarding the degradation of performance. My main concern relates to expectation management and ensuring that my colleagues in the operational areas of the business are aware of the impact, and likely future impact, of the slower response times.

2. Notwithstanding the above, it would have been possible for our pharmacist to expedite the dispensation of the prescription but, due to a lack of communication between our pharmacy staff, this was not done, leading to the situation you describe.

3. In the interim period cost elimination arising from the significant labour force reductions will protect the operating performance from the effects of poor utilisation of the installation teams.

4. He was conveyed to his place of residence in an intoxicated condition.

Preferred versions:

1. I am worried that my colleagues may not be fully aware of the effects of slower response times.

2. Our pharmacist should still have been able to dispense the prescription promptly, but there was a breakdown in communication.

3. The installation teams were not used as effectively as they should have been, but we saved money by shedding staff.

4. He was taken home drunk.

The last sentence was, in its original form, a classic example of police jargon. And we laugh because we recognise it. But it is far harder to recognise our own jargon because it has become second nature to us to use it.

Jargon

Here's a reminder of some common jargon, management-speak or bureaucratic language. Some of it may be pardonable in certain circumstances – but let's not forget the plain English alternative:

Jargon	Plain English
feedback	response, reaction
parameters	limits
implement	do, carry out
optimum	best
interface	meet, talk to
impact (verb)	affect
finalise	complete
input (noun)	contribution, ideas
input (verb)	suggest, say
output (noun)	results
relocate	move
in receipt of	have received
remit	pay in
funds	money
assistance	help
requirement	need
signage	signs
purchase	buy
prior to	before

10. *Don't be Vague*

THERE ARE MANY different ways of obscuring meaning. You can use abstractions, vague or unquantifiable terms, or the passive voice. All have a distancing effect. There are occasions when this is desirable, even essential, but it should not become a habit.

Abstractions

There is a strong temptation in management writing to make something sound more important – and more generally applicable – by moving from the concrete to the abstract. But in the process, it means you move from practice to theory.

This is how we acquire expressions like 'top-down direction, bottom-up input'. What a neat little concept it sounds! But what does it mean? We all know that top people direct – that's what executives are there for. And 'bottom-up input' surely just means that the people below them can have their say – and presumably be listened to? If you were to talk about bosses listening to their staff, that wouldn't sound half so impressive, would it? It certainly wouldn't qualify as management theory. But to ordinary people, it conjures up a far more vivid picture than 'top-down direction, bottom-up input'.

Almost everyone in business deals with customers or clients at some point. But in management circles, people tend to talk about 'customer feedback', the 'customer base' and 'client satisfaction'. You get the feeling that some of these people would do anything to avoid coming face to face with a real customer. Wouldn't it be more arresting, more meaningful, if someone wrote: 'A customer came up to me yesterday and said...' Suddenly, we're free of abstractions, back in the real world, talking in a way that connects directly to us.

In Chapter 7, we saw how quickly sentences could become bogged down when they began with abstract nouns. Abstractions in almost any form or context are the enemy of clarity – one of the most pervasive curses of corporate writing. Remember: if you want to speak to your reader, be specific.

Unquantifiable expressions

By being vague in your choice of words, you can avoid commitment; the more ambiguous you are, the harder it is for others to tie you down:

> *We have dealt with some major companies*
> *There will be significant changes*
> *Steps will be taken*
> *Every effort will be made*

Promises or statements such as these are easy to make and don't commit you to actual, positive action. If you cannot afford to tell the unvarnished truth – and let's face it, there are times when you can't – then by all means be vague. When you haven't enough information, you don't yet want to commit yourself, or you have to cover up for some mistake or omission, then you are obliged to blur the picture. But most of the time, it's a cop-out.

Consider this sentence from a broker's report on a French insurance company:

> *Although DEF has significant operations outside France, it has a large presence in the profitable French life market which provides the major influence on the group's results.*

There is not a lot to go on here – certainly not enough for a prudent investor who likes to be fully informed before committing money to a venture.

Note the three key words: 'significant'; 'large'; 'major'. What do they really mean in this context? One can only guess. Think how much more effective the following might have been:

> **Although DEF has offices in Paris, Rome and Stuttgart, it is its 30% share of the profitable French life market that accounts for most of the group's profits – $70.5m out of the $100.9m earned in the year ended April 1992.**

Now we have some hard facts which, combined with a respected professional opinion, might persuade us to invest in DEF. Now we can see how lazy the original writer was, erecting a screen of vague phrases to cover his lack of research.

If you care about meaning and want to communicate, words like the ones in the original report should set off alarm bells. If something is 'significant', what does it signify? If it is 'large', how large? And so on.

Use of the passive voice

Using the passive ('The report was written') rather than the active voice ('I wrote the report') is another common device designed – whether consciously or not – to muddy the waters. It shifts the emphasis onto the situation rather than the people responsible for it. By removing the personal touch it can also be used to intimidate and keep readers at a distance.

Consider these examples and note how the tone changes when expressed in the active voice:

Passive	Active
You will be notified in writing	**I'll write to you**
You will be collected at the airport	**We'll pick you up**

Using the active voice makes these sentences far less pompous and far more friendly.

In other instances, the passive voice simply allows the writer to avoid responsibility. In the following example the writer – or at least the body he represents – is to blame for failing to inform a student of the change in a deadline – but he manages to gloss over the point entirely:

> *You should have been informed of the new deadline but as you weren't, you will be granted another week in which to complete your assignment.*

By using the passive voice, repeating the word 'you' and using the word granted, the writer not only removes himself from the question of responsibility but almost makes the student feel that he is to blame.

Clearly, vague vocabulary and the passive voice are very useful if you want to keep things ambiguous, evade personal responsibility and avoid being tied down by your words. But if this becomes a habit in written business communications, you will soon appear confused, half-hearted, lacking in commitment, clarity, organisation and control. Compare the following:

Passive	Active
The decision was made	**I** made the decision
It was decided	**We** decided

Using the active voice conveys the impression that the writer has control of the situation and also establishes a human connection between writer and reader. It shows that the writer is prepared to take responsibility and that he is capable of decisive action when required.

Using the passive can, however, be useful when you want to emphasise the 'what' and gloss over the 'whom'. For example:

> *Your proposal was carefully considered but, in the end, it was felt that this would not be an appropriate line of action.*

In this case the identity of the person who actually considered and rejected the proposal is kept secret – and for a good reason. The writer doesn't want the rejected person to start pursuing personal vendettas against the person responsible. And so the decision is represented as having been made on the company's behalf. It is probably in everyone's interests to keep letters like these as impersonal as possible. It may be frustrating, but it is actually less hurtful to be rejected by an institution than by an individual.

How to avoid vagueness, while not saying too much

Let's not be too idealistic here. By all means avoid the abstract, the passive, the vague and the frankly cowardly. But do not feel obliged to say more than necessary – more than the reader genuinely needs to know and more than it is wise for you to reveal. There are times when the best of us must behave like politicians and dodge the question.

Someone from the customer complaints department of a leading clearing bank recently provided an example of the kind of tangle it is all too easy to get into. Responding to a customer's complaint about the time it took for a cheque to clear, he wrote:

> *Credits have to go through the clearing system and we do ask our customers to allow at least three working days. The Bank does not gain any real benefit from the money between this period since it is essentially in transit…*

You can sense that the writer is struggling to disguise the truth, can't you? How can he claim that the bank doesn't gain any 'real' benefit? Actually, it gains the benefit of possession of the customer's money for those three days – which presumably allows the bank to earn interest on the money markets. And what's wrong with that? Banks have to earn their money somehow. The writer kept plugging conscientiously on:

One could arguably construe the clearing system as being some-what antiquated in these days of electronic banking...

A favourite adage, often quoted in business as in politics, is: 'When you are in a hole, stop digging.' This is surely one of those occasions.

The best thing for the writer would have been to make as many valid and positive statements about the service the bank offers as possible, without being drawn into a detailed analysis of the situation:

The clearing system provides an opportunity for errors to be detected
OR
The clearing system ensures that all transactions are authenticated and checked
OR
The clearing system protects both payer and payee

Best of all, include a positive assertion such as:

There is no bank that clears cheques more quickly than we do.

As any general would confirm, it is sensible rather than ignoble to avoid battles on unfavourable ground.

11. *Style Points*

THIS CHAPTER CONTAINS guidelines, rather than rules. Many organisations have their own house styles, which may be different in certain details.

Abbreviations and acronyms

Do not use abbreviations unless the full word is very cumbersome or seems out of place written down. Use advertisement rather than ad, telephone rather than phone, television rather than TV, *Financial Times* rather than *FT*.

The BBC, however, is so well known that spelling it out as British Broadcasting Corporation is absurd. But there's no excuse for 'Beeb'. With other organisations frequently known by their initials, the general rule is to spell it out in the first instance, with the acronym in brackets afterwards; thereafter, you can use the initials, eg 'Department of Trade and Industry (DTI)' can subsequently be referred to as the DTI.

There's nothing wrong with acronyms. Nobody nowadays would bother to spell out Nato, or Radar. But be wary of inflicting your own internal acronyms on your readers – or, indeed, colleagues who may not be familiar with them.

Accents

A number of foreign words – particularly French ones like *rôle*, *façade*, *café* and *cliché* – have become so much a part of everyday English that they frequently appear without their accents. There is a case for keeping the accent on words like café and cliché since the accent alters the pronunciation. But just about everyone knows how they are pronounced, and it is no longer essential to keep the accents. With less well-known foreign expressions, like *mélange* and *résumé* (which would be particularly confusing without the accents), the best advice is to use an English word instead – 'mixture' and 'summary' would do equally well in this instance.

On the other hand, when you are quoting directly from a foreign language, or dealing with an overseas customer or contact, you should use the accents.

Americanisms

Where there are clear alternatives to the American versions, use English expressions. So, write 'companies' not 'corporations', 'districts' not 'neighbourhoods', 'car' not 'automobile', 'oblige'not 'obligate' and so on.

Look out for certain common US spellings and word forms. Select the English version unless you are writing for an American reader, or one more closely versed in American English.

English	American
defence (and other nouns ending -ence, like offence)	*defense, offense etc*
favour, endeavour etc	*favor, endeavor etc*
centre	*center*

For a comprehensive list of Americanisms, refer to *Fowler's Modern English Usage*.

Bullet points

Bullet points are good things – but you can have too much of a good thing. The idea behind them is that they should catch the eye. On a page consisting of five or six paragraphs of normal prose, three bullet points will instantly grab the attention. If there are six bullet points, there will not be so many paragraphs, and the bullet points will not stand out from the main text so well. Also, because there are six of them, they will not be so easy to take in and memorise. And if a whole page consists of bullet points – as I have often seen – they won't stand out at all; in such an instance, a paragraph of normal prose would stand out by breaking the monotony of the bullet points.

So if you want to use bullet points, make sure that you have at least two strong points to make, and never more than six.

The other vital consideration is that the bullet-pointed items should be clearly explained, and appropriately listed (see Listing, in Chapter 7).

Capitals

Capital letters should be used sparingly. Use them for proper names, place names and titles. Thus, Roger Jones might sign himself as 'Roger Jones, Marketing Manager'. But if we refer to Roger Jones as 'the marketing manager at the Biggin Hill branch', there is no need for capital letters. This applies to managing directors and chairmen, too – and, for that matter, prime ministers, dukes, or any office- or title-holder where their position is referred to in the general sense.

In the example above, we might want to use a capital B for Branch, to make it clear that we are talking about a particular branch – usually our own. But if there is no possible confusion, then keep it lower case.

He/she

In these politically correct times, we should try to avoid offending female readers by using the masculine gender throughout. But repeated use of he/she becomes irritating. The best solution is to use the plural wherever possible. For instance, if you write in a general sense about the reader, you may have to use 'he/she'. But if you refer to 'readers', you have no problem.

Just occasionally, you may want to use the singular noun in a general sense, to include both singular and plural. This is one instance when, to avoid the dreaded 'he/she', you can break the usual rules of subject/verb agreement and switch from 'customer' to 'they'.

As ever, the ultimate test is clarity and meaning. If it makes sense, then go ahead and break the rules.

Numbers

When you write a letter, you normally spell out single-figure numbers, but use numerals for 10 or more. For instance: 'You have three options...' But 'We have 57 different varieties.' (House style on this can vary.)

One exception is at the beginning of a sentence, where you would never use numerals (not least because a numeral after a full stop might look as if the point and the numeral were somehow related). So you would begin: 'A hundred years after the first branch was established at ...' A second exception is where you are using a succession of numbers, and it would look awkward to switch from prose to numerals. Then use numerals throughout – like football results.

The same applies to percentages. In normal prose, per cent should be spelled out. But if you are dealing with figures on a regular basis, this would soon look silly in a business context. So 'One account pays 6% interest, another 6.5%.'

Typefaces

Most letters should be written in the normal roman typeface. For internal memos and reports, you can be more creative, to make your message as clear as possible.

General guidance:

Bold Use to draw attention to a particular point or heading, and to emphasise it. Use bold for slogans, mottoes or phrases that are intended to linger in the memory.

Italic Use for technical terms (*andante, allegro* etc, in a musical context), for uncommon words in another language and to differentiate quotations from the rest of your text.

Underline Use for titles or headings.

12. *Troublesome Words and Phrases (an A-Z guide)*

Administer

Not 'administrate'. Better still, use 'run' or 'organise'.

Affect

'To have an effect on' (or, less commonly, 'to assume' or 'to put on'). Preferable to 'impact', now commonly used as a verb.

All right

Better than alright.

Alternate (adjective)

Means every other; so there should only be two 'alternatives'. If you want more, use 'options'.

& (ampersand)

Do not use '&' for 'and', except for company names eg 'Reckitt & Colman', 'Johnson & Johnson'.

And

Try to avoid having more than one 'and' in a sentence. And, although you can do it occasionally, you shouldn't make a habit of starting sentences with 'and'.

And/or

Avoid this expression, which is ugly and can be confusing. Better to spell out the options clearly.

As of

A pompous way of saying 'from' or 'since'. Please don't use it.

As such

A commonly misused expression. To be used properly, it must refer to something specific. The reader should be able to ask 'As what?' and get a clear answer. It makes no sense to use 'as such' in this instance:

> *The points you have made need to be carefully examined by my colleagues. As such, I have passed the letters to the executive office responsible for this matter.*

Instead of 'as such', the writer should have put 'consequently' or 'accordingly', or used some other linking phrase. Here is 'as such' used correctly:

> *Gemma Evans is entertainments manager. As such, she is responsible for social events throughout the year, notably the Christmas party.*

Beside

Means 'next to'; 'besides' means 'as well as'.

Biannual/biennial

Biannual means twice yearly whereas biennial means every two years. These expressions are very confusing, so don't use them.

Case

Frequently an unnecessary word. Prefer 'if' to 'in case…' And phrases like 'it is the case that…' can just be cut out altogether.

Circumstances

It should be 'in the circumstances', not 'under the circumstances'.

Cliche

Cliché is a French word that usually has an acute accent, but has become so anglicised that it often appears without its accent and doesn't need to be italicised. Cliches are occasionally useful because they sum something up, and are instantly recognised by the reader. But more often, they provoke a groan. Find your own way of saying something if you can.

Compare

If you are comparing similar things – like with like – you should 'compare with'. You might, for instance, compare the profit figures before tax *with* those after tax. Business people should not be comparing one thing to another – that's strictly for poets ('Shall I compare thee to a summer's day?').

Comprise

Means 'embrace the whole of'. 'The management team comprises X,Y and Z.' This means there is no one else in the management team. Should not be confused with 'include', but often is.

Considerable

A vague and useless adjective, which belongs with 'significant' – in the bin.

Consist

Same meaning as 'comprise', but requires the addition of the word 'of'. 'The management team consists of X, Y and Z.'

Current, currently

If the sentence is in the present tense, you hardly ever need 'current' or 'currently'. The only time it is useful is when you are contrasting what is happening 'currently' with what used to happen or what might happen in the future. But why not use 'now' instead?

Data

Prefer 'information'. Although 'data' is a shorter and increasingly popular word, it is not yet in widespread conversational use.

Decimate

Its original meaning is taken from the Roman practice of disciplining (and often executing) every tenth man in a legion after a defeat. Consequently it used to mean, and should mean, 'to lose a tenth'. But over the years, its meaning has become corrupted. Nowadays, most people use it when they mean 'destroy', 'slaughter' or 'annihilate'. Since its meaning has become so confused, it is best avoided.

Different

You can say 'different from' or 'different to', but 'from' is preferable – and logical, since one thing differs *from* another.

Disinterested

Frequently misused and confused with 'uninterested'. 'Disinterested' means 'having no material interest in', and hence 'impartial'. Uninterested simply means 'not interested'. You ask a 'disinterested' person to resolve a dispute; but you don't want such a person to be 'uninterested'.

Due to

This expression is problematical because of its several different meanings:

- Owed to, as in 'The sum of £100 is due to Mr X.'
- Scheduled to, as in 'The meeting is due to end at 4pm.'
- Caused by, because of, as in 'due to unforeseen circumstances ...'

It is in this last sense that 'due to' can cause confusion. Grammarians complain that it is usually used incorrectly, when the proper phrase is 'owing to'. But why use it anyway? It is much clearer to say 'because of' or 'as a result of...'

Earn, earnings

These can be confusing words, because 'earnings per share' comes under the heading of 'unearned income'. When 'earnings' really means 'profits', it is clearer to use 'profits'. It is possible, in the Machiavellian world of business, that in certain circumstances you may not want to be clear – in which case, you'll just have to assess the reader and the context, then use the appropriate word.

Effect

The noun resulting from the verb 'to affect'. There is also a verb, 'to effect', meaning to accomplish, or bring about: to effect a change. The expression 'in effect' means exactly what it says, which is much the same as 'in fact' or 'in practice'. 'Effectively' means 'with effect' – and that's a bit different. To do something 'effectively' means to do it well; to do something 'in effect' just means to do it.

E.g.

This means 'for example' (from the Latin *exempli gratia*). It should not be confused with 'ie', which means 'that is' (from the Latin *id est*). Neither should be used in normal prose, but only in footnotes or lists, where you don't want to repeat the words 'for example' or 'for instance'.

Essential(ly)

When you want to summarise something, 'essentially' is quite a useful word (meaning the same as 'in essence'), and more expressive than 'basically'. It is, however, equally liable to be misused to cover up lazy or vague writing. In business, we prefer to have things 'in detail', rather than 'in essence'.

Etc

A common abbreviation for the Latin *et cetera*, meaning 'and the rest'. It's a useful expression, but shouldn't normally be used in a formal letter, where it can look sloppy. In a report or internal memo, it will do.

Existing

This is one of those overused, padding words like 'current'. If you are writing about something in the present tense, it is usually clear that it exists. 'Existing' is only useful when being contrasted with 'past' or 'future'.

Facility

One of those horrible abstract nouns loved by bureaucrats and not used by normal people. A currency storage facility is a bank; if we offer currency exchange facilities, that means we can change foreign money. If the word 'facility' springs to mind, think again.

Factor

Another undesirable abstract noun. If something is a 'factor' in an equation, explain it in plain English. Consider the following sentence: 'Our training programmes are a vital factor in our success.' Plain English: 'We are more successful because we train people well.'

Former, latter
Avoid setting up a sentence or paragraph that juxtaposes one noun or adjective with another in this way; it usually sounds cumbersome.

Fortunately
See Presumptuous phrases on page 152.

Function
An ugly abstract noun. Avoid if you can, perhaps by using 'use' or 'purpose' instead.

Fund
This is what *The Economist Style Guide* says: 'Fund is a technical term, meaning to convert floating debt into more or less permanent debt at fixed interest. Do not use it if you mean to finance or pay for.' *The Economist* is only dealing with the verb, but even as a noun, it should be regarded as a technical banking term. When banks invite you to 'remit funds', they are really asking you to pay in money.

Get
A versatile word that is often used in sloppy constructions. There is no need for a task to 'get' done, when it can simply 'be' done. But if the word helps you 'get' from one point to the next clearly and effectively, and if the reader gets it, that's okay.

Holistic
Originally popularised as a medical term to describe treatment that went beyond conventional medicine to treat the whole person, physically and psychologically. Increasingly used by management consultants who like to think of themselves as enlightened company doctors.

Hopefully
This is an adverb, meaning 'full of hope'. You may travel 'hopefully'; you may fill in an application form 'hopefully';

you may write 'hopefully'. In due course, you will probably need to explain what you are hoping for, or your reader won't be any the wiser.

The word is commonly misused by being thrown in with some general assertion: 'Hopefully, the sun will shine tomorrow.' The sun can't hope, so this is literally nonsense. 'Hopefully' is most often used in this woolly, disconnected sense when the writer is not quite prepared to commit himself. 'We will meet again soon – hopefully' is not as definite as 'I hope we will meet again', and is thoroughly unconvincing; likely as not, the writer is hoping nothing of the sort. The best advice about 'hopefully' is not to use it.

However, nevertheless and therefore

'However' can be used in two senses. In the first sense, it means to whatever extent or in whatever way:

However hard I try, I never seem to get it right.
However you slice it, it always tastes the same.

This creates possible confusion when you want to use it in the second sense, which is by way of contrast with whatever went before. In this sense, it fulfils much the same function as but, but it requires different punctuation.

Here is an example of how NOT to use it:

Our internal policy framework is confidential, however, we ensure that guidelines are updated to refresh the message and clearly communicate policy to the appropriate staff.

When you read this for the first time, you are not immediately clear to which part of the sentence the 'however' belongs. The first part could easily be misread as a contrast with whatever went before. It is only when you read the rest of the sentence that you realise the 'however' belongs to the second half, contrasting with the first. The sentence doesn't work with this punctuation. It needs to be rewritten:

Our internal policy framework is confidential. We ensure, however, that guidelines are updated... OR **Our internal policy framework is confidential, but we ensure...**

The point about 'however' is that it is used to achieve a contrast with what went before, and the best way of doing this is to start a new sentence. You can't use 'however' in the middle of a sentence in the same way that you use 'but'. The same rule applies to 'nonetheless' (or 'nevertheless'), and 'therefore'. In many cases, you would be better off using 'but' or 'so', which are both much easier to use.

I

If you are writing on the company's behalf, 'we' is usually more appropriate. And if you are thinking of the reader, as you should be, the next most likely pronoun may well be 'you'. But there are times when you need to take responsibility. Much better, then, to say 'I will get in touch next week' or 'I will ensure that ...' than to use a passive construction. But you'd better keep your promise!

Impact

Should be used only as a noun. The verb, 'to impact', is an Americanism that has taken root among the fashion victims of corporate communications. There is no good reason to prefer it to 'affect', particularly since it often requires the addition of the unnecceary word 'on'.

Importantly

This is an adverb that can mean 'in an important manner'. For instance, 'The company chairman strode importantly into the room.' Unfortunately, the word has been so frequently misused when describing an action or situation that is important, or has important consequences, that it now has an alternative meaning. For instance: 'More importantly, he forgot to sign the cheque.' This ought to be wrong; he was not behaving in a more important manner when he forgot to sign the cheque. You should really say: 'More important, he forgot to sign the cheque.' Or find another way round it: 'What mattered more was that he forgot...' Anyway, 'importantly' – just like 'hopefully' – is now so widely misused that it is best avoided.

Inasmuch as; insofar as

Quaint and cumbersome expressions that can almost always be avoided.

In regard to, as regards

The second of these two expressions is easier to say, yet it is used less often than the first, which is cumbersome and sounds officious. In ordinary conversation, you would use 'as for' at the beginning of the sentence, or 'about' in the middle of the sentence. But 'as for' at the beginning of a sentence does not work so well on the page. Better to think again and rewrite the sentence. You need never use 'in regard to'.

Inter alia

This means 'among other things'. So why not use English instead of Latin?

In terms of

An awkward expression. Any sentence that contains 'in terms of' should almost certainly be rewritten.

In that

A cumbersome expression, best avoided.

Key

An overused word, as in 'key factors', 'key issues' etc. Try 'vital', 'essential', 'indispensable', just for a change. Or leave it out.

Late

The opposite of 'early'. Also used to mean 'dead'. Avoid expressions like 'of late' and 'lately'; they sound rather old-fashioned, and are too vague to be much use. Use 'recently' instead.

Latin words

If you studied Latin, you should have an advantage in dealing with words. But don't flaunt it. Prefer the Anglo-Saxon word to the Latin word every time.

Lay and lie

Can be confusing. 'Lay' is a transitive verb: to 'lay something down'. 'Lie' is intransitive: you may 'lie down', but you may not lie anything else down. But 'lay' is also the past tense of 'lie': 'I lay down.' 'Laid' is only the past tense of 'lay'; 'I laid my book on the table.' If you get confused, use 'put' instead of 'lay'.

Less/fewer

'Less' refers to quantity, 'fewer' to number. So you can have 'less tea, sugar or milk', but 'fewer cups, saucers and spoons'.

Do write 'less money' or 'less interest', but don't write 'less people' or 'less dividends'. You should say 'fewer people'; and you should say either 'lower dividends' or 'fewer dividends', depending which you mean.

Lest

Beginning to sound old-fashioned. Avoid it.

Loan

A noun that is occasionally used as a verb. Simpler to use it only as a noun. For the verb, use 'lend' instead.

Locate

An ugly word. Prefer 'find'. Also, prefer 'place' to 'location', and 'move' to 'relocate'.

Media

Is the plural of medium, and takes a plural verb. It covers press, TV and radio. The word can be overused – so don't use it if you can be more specific.

Metaphor

In business writing, there is little place for metaphors, let alone mixed ones. We don't, for instance, want to hear about a cloud with a silver lining that provides a window of opportunity.

Keep metaphors to a minimum. They can be expressive, but they can also tend towards cliché.

Monies

Banking parlance, not for public use. Keep money in the singular. If you need a plural, use 'sums' or 'amounts' instead.

Myself, yourself, etc

Some letter-writers like to use the intensive pronoun when it has no possible justification, eg 'If this is convenient to yourself' or 'Please return the form to myself.' This makes any lover of English cringe. See Pronouns in Chapter 7.

Nice

A vague, more or less useless word, not suitable for business writing.

Nouns

Particularly abstract ones, are favoured by writers who want to sound important rather than communicate. Nounitis is one of the most debilitating diseases in corporate literature, and can only be counteracted by frequent injections of verbs.

Obviously

See Presumptuous phrases on next page.

One

'One' is not inclined to use this pronoun much these days. Depending on the context, 'you' or 'we' is likely to be more appropriate.

Ongoing

Is an ugly and unnecessary word that became fashionable in business writing in the 1970s and is now declining in use. Use 'continuing' instead.

Oriented

There is no need for the extra syllable of 'orientated'. But either way, it's not the most elegant way of phrasing something. 'Inclined' would be better in most contexts.

Over/under

When talking about numbers, prefer 'more than' and 'less than'.

Personal, personally

The 'personal' touch is one thing, usually a good way of dealing with customers. 'Personal' opinion may be less appropriate; customers would prefer a 'professional' opinion.

Prepositions

Pedants insist that you should never end a sentence with a preposition – and they are right most of the time. But it was overprecise and pedantic writing that prompted Churchill to remark: 'This is the kind of English up with which I will not put.'

Presently

This has two meanings. It can be the same as 'currently' – at present – or it can mean 'soon': 'He will be with you presently.' For this reason, it is best avoided.

Presumptuous phrases

'*You will, of course, be aware…*' If the reader *is* aware, is this worth repeating? And if they are *not* aware, then why not? You have just implied that they should be. If you have good reason for inserting this phrase – to remind someone who shouldn't need reminding, for instance – then by all means use it. But if you have any doubts, it might be better simply to recap the position as you understand it.

'*We fully understand your position…*' Readers are liable to take issue with this. They might well think: 'Oh, no, you don't. How could you? You don't know anything about me.' Stick to the facts eg 'In your letter of September 4th, you told us…'

'*You will, I am sure, be pleased…*' How do you know?

'*Obviously…*' Obvious to whom? If it's obvious to you, but not to your reader, this suggests obtuseness or ignorance on their part. If it is obvious to both of you, then why are you bothering to mention it?

'*Fortunately/unfortunately…*' For whom? And is it really a matter of fortune? Luck should scarcely come into a business relationship.

Real, really

'Real' is the opposite of 'imaginary'. Don't use it without good reason, or as a general intensifier, as in: 'We're really delighted that at last Bill has scored a real success.'

Regretfully, regrettably

Regrettably, these can get confused. 'Regretfully' is subjective, and suggests that the subject of the sentence is full of regret. 'Regretfully, he trudged away, his head down.' 'Regrettably' is used objectively, in the sense that something is to be regretted.

Relative, relatively

These words must only be used when a clear comparison is being made. You should not say 'There are relatively few people here' unless you are contrasting this, for instance, with the number that were here last year, or the much larger number assembled next door. 'Our High Street offices have 100 staff. The Tavistock Road branch is relatively small, having only 15 staff.'

Remit, remittance

When talking of money, these are bankers' words, not customers' words. Prefer 'pay in', and 'deposit' or 'cheque', depending on the context. 'Remit' has other meanings, too. It can mean 'area of responsibility', as in 'within my remit'. 'Remittal' is a legal term for referring a case to another court. And 'remission' means forgiveness or 'easing'; a patient can enjoy remission from a disease, or a convict can benefit from remission of sentence. Because of all these different meanings, you might be better off using another word.

Respective, respectively

Use of these words seems pedantic nowadays. Avoid them if you can.

Significant

A useful adjective for statisticians who wish to differentiate between emerging trends and mere blips. Useless in almost any other context. Instead of describing something as significant, say what it signifies.

Slang

Slang should be treated like jargon, with care. Occasionally, a slang expression is uniquely expressive, but whether you should use it or not depends on the context and the reader.

So

So should not be overused as an intensifier, eg 'We're so pleased...' But as a conjunction, it is usually preferable to 'therefore'. It is certainly easier to use.

Some

Avoid using this vague adjective if you can be more specific. And don't use it to mean 'about', as in 'Some 300 people were there.'

Special

'Special' was one of the first adjectives to be extensively abused by advertisers, and is no longer as special as it used to be.

Split infinitives

The split infinitive is an obsession with some people. It need not bother the rest of us too much. The rule is that when you use the infinitive tense – 'to go', for instance, you should not put any word in between. So the famous mission of the *Starship Enterprise* 'to boldly go where no man has gone before' is one of the most resounding split infinitives of modern times.

To split an infinitive is usually ugly and almost invariably unnecessary. To deliberately split an infinitive is, however, the surest way to thoroughly annoy one of those pedantic people who care about rules more than they care about meaning.

Substantial

A catch-all word best avoided. If it is 'substantial', what is its substance? And if you just mean 'large', then write 'large'.

Superlatives

Can *very* easily be overused, so that they cease to be effective.

Synergy

A pretentious word meaning 'working together'. Avoid if possible.

Table

By all means use a table as an illustrative device which also helps to break up text. Don't use 'table' as a transitive verb. In English it means 'to put forward', as in 'tabling a motion'. In American English 'tabling a motion' means ruling it out: it means exactly the opposite.

Target

Is much happier as a noun. Instead of 'targeting' something, why not 'aim' or 'direct'?

Than

When making a comparison, make sure you clearly identify the two objects of comparison. 'I'm closer to my brother than my sister' is not clear. Do you mean 'I'm closer to my brother than to my sister' or 'I'm closer to my brother than my sister is?' You have to spell it out.

Thanking you in anticipation

No thanks. Keep your expressions of gratitude direct and natural. Don't write 'I thank you' or 'We thank you...' Just 'Thank you...'

That or which

'Which' has various specific uses. For instance, when you offer a choice: which of two options will you take? Or when you refer to a particular thing, or item, or place, eg 'Chipping Camden, which is one of the most beautiful towns in the Cotswolds...'

In other contexts, 'which' and 'that' are frequently inter-changeable, so don't waste time agonising over which to choose. On the whole, 'that' is more versatile, and there are one or two constructions in which only that will do: 'Is there anything 'that' needs to be done?' 'It is the company that must decide.'

Time

Unless your house style insists otherwise, don't write out 'o'clock'; and don't use the 24-hour clock (unless you are in the armed forces). Use numerals, and add 'am' or 'pm', without spaces or points: 'I will see you at 2pm on Thursday.'

Try to

Not 'try and'.

Unique

Means 'one and only'. So it cannot be qualified by 'more', 'less', 'almost' or 'rather'.

Utilise

Prefer 'use'.

Vacation

An American word; 'holiday' is English.

Venue

Prefer 'place'.

Verbal

Is not the same as 'oral'. If you mean 'spoken', as opposed to 'written down', use 'oral'.

While

'While' is preferable to 'whilst', 'among' to 'amongst'.

Would

Why would anyone want to use the apologetic, ingratiating conditional tense? 'I would ask you to bear in mind that...' 'I would mention that...' 'I would like to take this opportunity to...' 'I would like to assure you that...' are introductory phrases that can simply be cut out. Stop pussy-footing around and get to the point.

PART IV

The Right Result

13. *Model Letters*

SALES

Model letter 1

High Street Bakery

21 High Street, Middle Vantage, Gloucestershire PE21 5BL

1 July 1998

Dear Mrs Jones

We are proud to announce the reopening, under new ownership, of the High Street Bakery on 1 September. On that day, and for the rest of the month, we will be offering free loaves in exchange for one of the three FREE LOAF vouchers enclosed with this letter. We hope this will give you an opportunity to try some of the many different kinds of bread we will be stocking.

The High Street Bakery has always been famous for its farmhouse, cottage, wholemeal and granary loaves, and we will continue to make those to the same recipe. We will also be offering a number of speciality breads, including baguette, ciabatta, focaccia, rye and sourdough. And of course, there will be pastries, cakes and pies.

You may well recognise several of the staff. Laura Hopkins, who served at the old bakery for 14 years, will resume her place behind the counter. John Roberts, formerly assistant baker, steps up to become one of two head bakers.

If you would like to open – or reopen – an account at the bakery, arrange deliveries, or make suggestions or enquiries, please drop in any time, or give us a call at the number at the top of this letter.

We look forward to seeing you, and serving you.

Yours sincerely

Edna Todd

Managing Director

INTRODUCTION

Model letter 2

Thomas Jones Associates
Parkway House, 39 Main Street, Norwich NO1 9LP

James Morris
15 The Firs
King's Lynn
Norfolk

1 September 1998

Dear James

I was delighted to hear about your success with the buy-out. You said you needed to hire an accountant, and I mentioned our accountant, Adrian Shadbolt.

I have since contacted Adrian, and mentioned that you might be interested in his services. It turns out that he has advised on several management buy-outs, most recently the one in which Shoe Shuffle of Leicester negotiated its independence from the World Footwear Company.

It sounds to me as if Adrian could be just the man for you. We've got to know him quite well over the time he has worked for us, and he is a pleasure to deal with – a thoroughly soothing presence, and with a good sense of humour, too.

I told him you might have sorted someone else out, so he won't be expecting a call, but he won't be surprised to get one either. His phone number is 01555 202021. Over to you.

The best of luck with whatever you do.

Yours sincerely

Thomas Jones

REFERENCE

Model letter 3

Ryan Communications
172 Southampton Road, Portsmouth PO2 9JA

30 June 1998

To whom it may concern

Harry Cook started his cleaning company, Whizzalong, in 1993, and has turned it from a three-person operation into a successful company employing 20 people and serving some of the best corporate clients in Dursley. He is an old friend of mine, and I can vouch for his honesty and reliability.

He has run the cleaning of our offices for the past four years, and we have no anxieties about giving him and his staff access to everything but the personal drawers of people's desks. I know that Harry vets all his employees very carefully.

In addition, his staff are exceptionally conscientious. We frequently leave notes requesting that attention be paid to some particular item, and if this requires the purchase of special cleaning materials, Whizzalong regard this as part of their job.

If you have any queries about their work, please contact me any time at this address. I recommend Whizzalong unreservedly.

Yours sincerely

Jonathan Brown

Managing Director

INVITATION

Model letter 4

Christopher Noble

17 The Rise, Worcester

Peter Bridge
Chairman
A1 Motors Plc
Warwick Business Park
Birmingham
B15 8RZ

24 July 1998

Dear Mr Bridge

I heard you speak at this year's CBI conference and I resolved there and then to try to persuade you to address the Worcester Round Table. Now the opportunity has arrived.

Your name is top of our list for one simple reason: I don't believe anyone knows so much about the car industry in the West Midlands. Among our members we have several men and women whose companies supply goods or services to the major vehicle manufacturers in this area, and I know they would be fascinated to hear your views about the future of the industry, and have the opportunity to ask a few questions.

As you may know, the Round Table is not in a position to pay guest speakers. Nonetheless, our annual dinners have attracted some notable guests in recent years, including Sir Michael Edwardes and Robert Horton.

We offer a truly excellent dinner – the Royal Oak Hotel being a new entry in this year's *Good Food Guide* – and a double room for you and your wife if you would like to stay the night. We would be honoured if you would both come.

We usually hold our annual dinners in the middle of the week, in early September, so if you are able to accept, please let me know as soon as possible and we will fix a date. Finally, the timing of your address would be entirely up to you. Most of our guests opt to speak after the main course, but more than one has opted to speak before dinner, on the grounds that this makes the meal more enjoyable. The choice is yours.

I hope you can make space in your diary for the Worcester Round Table. I know that you will rarely find a more appreciative audience.

Yours sincerely

Christopher Noble

Speaker Co-ordinator

APPLICATION

Model letter 5

July 1st 1998

Sarah James
29 Cathedral Close
Exeter
EX2 1JB

Karen Foot
Personnel Manager
AMP Computers
10 Hillcrest Park
Exeter EX4 5BZ

Dear Miss Foot,

You advertised in the latest issue of the *Daily Telegraph* for a business development manager to market your products in the south-west of Britain, and I should like to be considered for the post.

I know your software very well, and admire it. In 13 years of working in computer services, most recently as a freelance consultant, I have sold many of your products. Having worked for Apple computers in Los Angeles from 1989–91, I also know what it is like to work for an American employer, and I enjoy the culture of challenge.

Finally, I believe that I should be able to offer you one crucial advantage: not only do I know the area well, having lived here in Exeter for just over five years; I also know many of the key players in the industry. You may assess my other qualifications from the curriculum vitae enclosed with this letter.

I hope you will be kind enough to see me.

Yours sincerely

Sarah James

REQUEST

Model letter 6

1 September 1998

The New Gymnasium – Nearly There!

Dear Parent

Building on the new gymnasium – a project dear to many of us who have been organising fund-raising events for the past few years – is due to start in March.

The good news is that the project has received approval for a lottery grant of £25,000. The bad news is that we are still £5,000 short of the money the school is required to raise.

If we can raise this money now, we can be sure that by the beginning of the autumn term, when building work should be complete, we will not only be able to use the gym, but will be able to fill it with all the equipment (not just ropes, rings, bars and vaulting horses but also a table-tennis table and stackable chairs) that will enable it to be used for the maximum benefit of every child in the school.

A plaque will be displayed immediately inside the gym listing the names of every person who donates or raises £100 or more. But whatever you can give will make a difference: £10 will buy six clothes pegs, £20 will buy two table-tennis bats and balls.

This is the first and last time we shall be making a direct appeal for donations. Our fund-raising efforts will continue, notably at the school's summer fete on 15 June. But we do need to put money in the bank account now. So please give what you can. Just send a cheque payable to the 'St Peter's Gymnasium Fund', or fill in the tear-off slip with your credit card details. A stamped, addressed envelope is enclosed.

Whatever you send will make a difference, helping to ensure that our children have the means of staying fit and healthy during their time at St Peter's.

Yours sincerely

Martin Jefferson

Chairman PTA

CHASING

Model letter 7

Alan Hudson Roofing
Chappell Road, Blackburn, Lancashire BL6 4OF

2 August 1998

Valerie Rudge
Managing Director
XYZ Company
Archibald Road
Blackburn
BB1 2NJ

Non-payment of Invoice No 1598

Dear Ms Rudge

In spite of repeated reminders sent to Charles Nash in your accounts department, your company has failed to settle this account. I enclose copies of previous correspondence, which has been strictly one-way. We have received no communication whatsoever from your company since this work was completed on 29 June.

As I am sure you will appreciate, we cannot ignore this debt any longer. If we do not hear from you within 10 days of the date on this letter, the matter will be placed in the hands of our solicitors.

Yours sincerely

Alan Hudson

Managing Director

COMPLAINT

Model letter 8

Super 8 Videostore
12 High Street, Northallerton, Yorks

Reg Garside
Managing Director
AV Video Supplies
15 Montford Place
Thirsk, Yorks

12 July 1998

Dear Reg

We have done business together for three years now, and I hope you would agree that it has been a mutually profitable relationship. So I'm sorry to have to write to you now as a thoroughly dissatisfied customer.

Yesterday was the third time in the past two months in which our orders from you were not fulfilled. On the first two occasions, some items arrived but not others. Then yesterday, when we were expecting 15 videos in all, the whole order seems to have gone missing. I have enclosed a copy of the fax that was sent to your office last Friday, ordering the 15 videos. When we rang to check that the order had been received, Steve, our regular contact in the order department, confirmed that it had. But Yvonne in Dispatch, whom we contacted yesterday when the order didn't arrive, said she knew nothing about it.

Whoever was responsible, the mix-up was at your end – and it wasn't a one-off. This latest episode caused us considerable embarrassment with customers who turned up expecting the videos we promised them today. It is simply not good enough, Reg, and we need to know that you are doing something to rectify the situation, or we shall have no choice but to search for another supplier.

In the circumstances, I trust you will feel able to fulfil this same order without further delay, and free of charge.

I hope you can sort this problem out, and we can return to the smooth business relationship we enjoyed until very recently.

Yours sincerely

Jack Duffield

Proprietor

CONDOLENCE

Model letter 9

'Hillholme', 34 Digby Rise, Bedford, MK40 2JY

Arthur Prescot
19 St David's Road
Bedford
MK40 9ZB

12 August 1998

Dear Arthur

I called your office this morning and heard the dreadful news about your father. This must have been a great shock. Having seen him with you only three weeks ago, I find it hard to believe.

Your dad was just a perfect gentleman, so friendly, so charming, so keen to put strangers at their ease. It was always a pleasure to hear his voice on the telephone, or be greeted by him at your door. He bore the pain of his arthritis with great bravery, and although it must have been hard work sometimes looking after him, I know you and Lorna will miss him very much.

I told Sheila the news, and she joins me in sending all our sympathy and best wishes to you, Lorna and the whole family.

Yours

Jeremy

INFORMATION

Model letter 10

Tyler plc
Tyler House, 497 Piccadilly, London W1 9DY

2 August 1998

Dear Shareholder

In the first half of this year, our company has recorded a trading loss of £93,000. This appears to be a disappointing result, particularly when compared with a profit for the previous six months of £255,000. But such a comparison is thoroughly misleading, taking no account of two exceptional factors.

Just five months ago, the company installed a new software programme to handle all accounts and inventory, at a cost of £200,000. Normally, we would have phased the payment for this software, but this would have cost us more; we obtained a 25% discount on the understanding that we paid immediately, which, thanks to some careful husbandry over previous years, we were comfortably able to do.

The second exceptional circumstance was, as you may know, a fire at the main warehouse a mere two weeks later. This was the first serious fire we have sustained in 20 years, and it meant that orders could not be fulfilled for three and a half weeks. Apart from the extensive damage, there was a knock-on effect on business that is still being assessed. When the insurance pay-out is agreed – which we anticipate will happen within the next six months – that will have a positive effect on the figures roughly equivalent to the negative effect the fire had in the first place.

In these circumstances, it is extremely difficult to put the past six months into context. There was a slight fall in demand, but this was in line with industry trends.

Finally, it is worth mentioning that the installation of the new systems has meant we need fewer administrative staff. Three weeks ago, we embarked on a programme of cutbacks that will eventually reduce our headcount by 15%.

All in all, then, we have no reason to feel despondent about the future. Indeed, I can say with some confidence that we expect to return to profit over the coming six months.

In the event of any dramatic developments, we shall keep you informed.

We look forward to welcoming you to the annual meeting on 26 June, when there will be further opportunities to analyse our situation.

Yours sincerely

Donald Tyler

Chairman

DECLINING INVITATION

Model letter 11

122 Henderson Avenue, Sevenoaks, TNS 3SB

15 September 1998

Angela Johnson
Anderson Brothers Ltd
St Peters House
23 High Street
Dartford
Kent DA6 4TE

Dear Angela

Bad news, I'm afraid. We can't make your party on the 28th, as I shall be on my way to Amsterdam for a sales conference. We shall both be very sorry to miss it, but I hope it goes well anyway. Thanks for thinking of us. I'll give you a call as soon as I'm back.

Yours

Jennifer Lyle

REJECTION

Model letter 12

Morris Jeffries plc
29–33 St James' Street, Leicester LE7 INQ

Christopher Thorpe
16 Villiers Close
Market Harborough
Leics

20 September 1998

Dear Christopher

We greatly enjoyed meeting you on Tuesday, and you created a thoroughly positive impression. Alas, we had only two vacancies, and you are one of the people we have to disappoint – for the moment, at least.

In most years, your personal qualities and academic qualifications would have won you a place on our management trainee scheme. But this was an exceptional year, and you were beaten by two exceptional applicants – one with an outstanding university degree, the other with all the essential qualifications, and some completed project work proving her aptitude beyond question.

It would be unfair to raise your expectations and, in your own interest, you should certainly apply for jobs elsewhere. If, however, you do not find a permanent position, I hope you will keep us in the back of your mind. There is nothing for you here at the moment, but if you should find some worthwhile short-term project, by all means contact us again when you have completed that work. With more experience under your belt, you would certainly have a strong claim to join the management trainee scheme at a later stage.

We wish you the best of luck, whatever option you choose to pursue in the immediate future.

Yours sincerely

Michael Humphries

Human Resources Manager

REFUSAL

Model letter 13

The Gift Shoppe
24 Parkway, Chichester, W. Sussex CH3 4LR

17 January 1998

Dear Mrs Reed

Thank you for your letter of 12 January 1998. I can imagine how disappointed you must have been to find out that the bookshelves you bought from us a fortnight ago were not the kind your mother had wanted.

I'm afraid, however, that our policy – displayed in a frame above the counter for our customers' attention – is to give refunds only if goods sold turn out to be faulty, damaged or somehow mis-represented by their packaging. In this case, the store was not at fault, but we sympathise with your situation. Although we can't give you a refund, we can suggest two other possibilities, one of which I hope will suit you.

Assuming you still have the receipt, you're welcome to exhange the shelves for anything else in the store. If the item you choose is cheaper than the one you're exchanging, then we'll give you a credit note for the difference, valid for 12 months. If, on the other hand, you can't find anything you need or want from our present stock, or would prefer to wait until a later date to choose, we will be happy to give you a credit note for the full amount. This will be valid for a year, during which time I'm confident you will be able to find a good use for it.

Whichever option you choose, we look forward to seeing you at our store again, and will be happy to help you in any way we can.

Yours sincerely

Margaret Dickens

Proprietor

RESIGNATION

Model letter 14

17 Shakespeare Crescent
Colchester
Essex
CO3 2NN

14 July 1998

Dear Ron

As you know, I shall be leaving Wolstenhome Bros on 31 July this year, and I am enormously grateful to you for being prepared to waive one month of my statutory notice period.

Much as I look forward to my new job at Hobbit & Co – and it really was an offer I couldn't refuse – I shall have mixed feelings about leaving. It's been an eventful six years, in which we have, I like to think, done some pretty good work together. For my part, I have certainly learned a lot from you, as I have from many of my colleagues.

I shan't be that far away, and I hope I'll be allowed back occasionally! I look forward to telling you all what life is like on the other side of the Pennines.

With best wishes to you and Deirdre.

Yours ever

Edward Morrison

REPRIMAND

Model letter 15

Harmony Public Relations
12 Temple Street, Bristol BS2 5OX

Richard Twiggett
17 Clifton Road
Bristol
BS3 6TM

12 April 1998

Dear Richard

Yesterday was not the first time you have come back from lunch obviously the worse for drink. Of course we like to entertain clients, and from time to time we may drink a glass or two more than we should. If we allow this to happen, the least we can do in the afternoon is to stay out of the way, so that others can get on with their work. But you don't seem to be able to do this. Two weeks ago I had to insist you tone down your conversation on the admin floor after lunch. Now, having received complaints from two members of staff about your behaviour yesterday, I am obliged to give you an official warning. If it happens again, you will be dismissed.

I don't want to lose you, so I hope you take this letter seriously, and clean up your act. Your work for this company over the past five years has made you enormously valuable to us, and your bonus last September was well earned. Please don't throw it all away.

If there are deeper personal problems, please tell me as much as you can about them, and I will do my best to help. We want nothing more than to have you back in harness, adding your unique enthusiasm and vitality to the team's work. But we need you sober. Then, in a year's time, we can strike this letter from the record.

Yours sincerely

James Browning

Managing Director

APOLOGY

Model letter 16

Westland Bank plc
839 Regent Street, London W1X 9PT

12 June 1998

Dear Mr Preston

I was extremely sorry to hear about your experiences last week, which clearly arose as a result of an error on the bank's part.

I have investigated this episode, and it seems that one of our lending officers was momentarily distracted while processing a number of accounts, and simply typed in the data from someone else's account, with the result that you thought you were well within your overdraft limit when in fact you had gone £200 over. Mistakes like this are extremely rare, and the member of staff concerned was extremely upset to discover his error; it was the first he had committed in 10 months in the department. We have done all we can to ensure that it won't happen again.

In the circumstances, and in the view of the embarrassment this must have caused you when trying to make a withdrawal, I have arranged for your account to be credited with £50 – the amount you intended to withdraw last week.

Your account is now in order, and I hope this uncharacteristic error will not harm your relationship with the bank.

Please give me a call if there is anything more I can do.

Yours sincerely

Alexander Neale

Chief Executive

14. *Model Reports*

Executive summary

Sutherlands (45 Lexington Street, London W1. Tel 0171 434 3401). Highest new entry in *Good Food Guide*. Self-consciously trendy decor with hideous mirrors. Excellent service. Outstanding food. Starters include sensational lobster ravioli. Inventive main courses, particularly good on game. Smallish portions. Fine English cheeses.

Two-course menu at £21.50; surprise menu at £37.50; house wines £8–11

Minutes

Extracts from Hansard dated 23 February 1998

Questions to Mr Keith Bradley, Parliamentary Under-Secretary of State for Social Security

Mr Bradley: In 1998-99, we expect the agency to clear about 560,000 maintenance applications, an increase of more than 56% compared with the number cleared in 1996-97.

The agency is reorganising itself over the next year to move more staff on to front-line work and to improve telephone contact with customers. In addition, it will centralise work that does not require face-to-face contact with the public.

Those changes will allow the agency to increase staffing levels by

300 by March 1999 while saving £5 million in administrative expenditure.

Mr Russell: The Minister of State said earlier that Parliament had sleepwalked[1] into the nightmare of the CSA. Is it not time to stop the Rip van Winkle approach to the CSA, bearing in mind that in one year Members of Parliament deal with 18,000 cases? Will the Government provide additional staff to ease the workload of Hon. Members dealing with CSA cases?

Mr Bradley: Rip van Winkle woke up on 1 May. The Government are undertaking a thorough review of the CSA, as my Right Hon. Friend the Minister of State explained. We will present proposals in the summer and the points raised by the Hon. Gentleman will form part of the review.

[1] As Matthew Parris noted in the *The Times*, Mr Russell actually said 'slepwalked', but there is no such word so Hansard edited Mr Russell

Analysis report

Argentina in 1998

Executive summary

Argentina's prospects at the beginning of 1998 are encouraging. Democratic politics look more firmly rooted than ever, the economy has grown steadily since 1995, and beef farming heads a growing list of successful industries. Main plus points:

- Fastest-growing economy in Latin America – probably 7% this year.
- Inflation and unemployment falling.

On the downside, there is still a huge gulf between rich and poor, and no properly developed business or financial services sector. Corruption pervades almost every walk of life, from daily financial dealings to top-level politics. Minus points:

- Average real incomes now only 4% higher than they were in 1974.
- Only 60% of taxes owed are actually collected.

Economy

Argentina's economy has emerged strongly from the 1995 recession caused by the collapse of the Mexican peso in 1995. Gross domestic product in the third quarter of 1997 was 8.6% up on the same period the previous year. Inflation, 5,000% in 1991, is now negligible. Unemployment, having more than doubled between 1993 and 1996 to 18%, is back down to 14%.

The foundations of the modern Argentine economy were laid in 1991 when, alongside widespread privatisation and deregulation, the peso was linked to the US dollar, and backed by foreign exchange reserves. The newly convertible currency survived the 1995 crisis, and once it had proved its durability in this way, international investors began to see Argentina as a good bet. The country's current recovery is led by investments (up more than 20% in 1997) and exports (up 10% in 1997) rather than consumption (up only 5.6%, compared with 5.2% the previous year). Consequently, there is not yet any significant rise in living standards. Indeed, despite growth of 28% since 1990, average real incomes have risen only 2% since 1974.

Growth is expected to be around 7% in 1997, 20% over the next three years, with the prospect of a continuing fall in unemployment. In 1998 the government hopes to reduce the budget deficit to $3.5 billion, down from $4.5 billion in 1997, just within the limits set by the IMF. Although prospects are generally good, they could be upset by a slowdown in the Brazilian economy, or by a recurrence of civil unrest, a result of the huge gap between rich and poor.

Politics

Fifteen years on from the military dictatorship that led the country to defeat in the Falklands, Argentina has a functioning and apparently stable democracy. The Peronist President Carlos Menem won almost 50% of the vote in 1995, and has now been in power for eight years. His economic reforms, however, have not yet brought widespread prosperity or popularity, and his administration has begun to be tainted by corruption allegations. The justice minister resigned last June after newspapers exposed links between government ministers and the postal entrepreneur Alfredo Yabran. There is little public confidence in the judiciary, which is dominated by Menem appointees.

Social protests grew more fervent in 1997, with demonstrators in the provinces demanding jobs, while teachers went on hunger strike to reinforce their demands for more money for education. Mr Menem's approval ratings are down to 18%, and he may well lose his party's presidential nomination for 1999. Opposition to the Peronists remains divided, and there is a broad consensus behind the programme of economic liberalisation and continuing privatisations. Trade unions retain considerable influence, however, and attempts to achieve labour flexibility have fallen a long way short of what the IMF has been urging.

Abroad, the Menem regime has gradually toned down its initially pro-American policy, and is giving increasing support to its colleagues within Mercosur, the free trade group comprising Argentina, Brazil, Uruguay, Paraguay, Chile and Bolivia. Diplomatic relations with Britain have been reopened, but little progress has been made on fishing or oil prospecting rights around the Falkland Islands.

Industry

Beef farming is the traditional mainstay of the economy, and remains the most important ingredient in agro-industry exports that were worth $8.8 billion in 1996 – nearly twice as much as six years earlier. Argentine beef is fed on grass, giving it the dual advantage of being free from BSE and not susceptible to fluctuations in grain harvests. Sheep farming is on the decline, but forestry in the north has been attracting investor interest, and the wine industry is showing promise. Land values have more than doubled in the past 10 years.

Argentina has reserves of minerals that have barely been exploited. Mining, a marginal activity in the 1980s, has been given a fillip by recent economic stability and a change in the mining law. Mining registered its first trade surplus in 1997, and mineral exports could reach $1.3 billion by the year 2000. The country's biggest mining project is the Alumbrera gold and copper mine in the north-west province of Catamarca. In the same area, production has just begun on a mine which is ultimately expected to supply up to 30% of the world's demand for lithium.

Business and finance

Corruption is as pervasive in business as it is in politics, with journalists routinely being paid to write favourable stories, and even the local branch of IBM accused of paying $37 million to secure a $249 million contract with the state-owned Banco Nacion. Argentina as yet has no shareholder culture to regulate the behaviour of company bosses.

Many banks are still small and undercapitalised, but the Spanish are leading a wave of investment in banking which promises to provide a more solid financial infrastructure. Liquidity requirements are being increased and supervision stepped up, and the central bank is moving to eradicate the problem of bad debt.

US-led private equity funds are beginning to invest in agro-industry, services and energy, but the financial sector remains chronically underdeveloped. Private pension funds are in their infancy.

Report with recommendations

Nowheeze   Sector: Pharmaceuticals   Share price: 163p

GREAT NEWS FOR ASTHMA SUFFERERS

Last Friday, **Nowheeze**, which has developed a revolutionary asthma treatment, got the all-clear from the US authorities to begin clinical trials of its new inhaler, a high-pressure spray that relieves asthma symptoms immediately, without any side effects.

Nowheeze floated last September, raising £28m. Its product, Freeflow, uses the newly developed drug Zinovil, in combination with a mild anaesthetic, in a spray that instantly relaxes muscles in the throat and lungs, allowing the patient to breathe with freedom. Zinovil is not a steroid, and in three years of trials in Europe, the drug has shown no side effects whatsoever.

Risk to investors is low because **Nowheeze** is using drugs that have already been approved by European medical authorities, and because it has a strong intellectual rights position, which should prevent other companies penetrating the market.

Besides Freeflow, **Nowheeze** is developing a pill for the treatment of bronchitis, and a spray, again using Zinovil, which is believed to be effective in relieving the common cold. The potential for this company is enormous, and it may well be able to claim a hefty market share in a matter of months.

Nowheeze is already working with three of the top five pharmaceutical companies in the world, and there are rumours of further deals in the pipeline. Trial results for Freeflow are expected in the US by the end of June.

BUY NOW

Market value: £102m

Ord price: 189p   *12-month high:* 189p Low: 141p

Net asset value: 35p   *Net cash:* £18.6m

Year to 31 March	Turnover	Pre-tax Profit £m	Stated Earnings per share (p)	Net Dividend per share (p)
1995	0.34	−0.12	–	nil
1996	0.29	−0.39	–	nil
1997	0.34	−2.46	–	nil

15. *Model E-mail*

Model e-mail 1

FROM: David
TO: Gina
SUBJECT: Urgent thought

Fantastic presentation. Sorry I had to leave early. One thought struck me though. What happens if we go ahead with the new software and the merger doesn't happen? I really think we ought to have some kind of fall-back position. Maybe you've already thought of this, but I think we need to spell it out before we present it to the board. Can we meet first thing on Monday? Give me a call over the weekend on 01222 567890.

Model e-mail 2

FROM: Jane Bowen janebow@ferdinand.co.uk
TO: Tim Fowler tim.fowler@starbike.com
SUBJECT: Whizbike marketing strategy

Dear Tim

Thank you for all the material you gave me about the Whizbike. It sounds like a sensational machine, and we would very much like to help you make it a success.

You asked me for a quick reaction and estimate for producing a detailed marketing strategy. I have yet to discuss this with my colleague Trevor Kirby, who has some experience in bicycle manufacture, but I've arranged to see him on Monday, so we could start work in earnest then. I am pretty confident that we could devote enough time to the project to have a strategy document ready for you by the following Monday.

In the meantime, a few preliminary observations:

- The Whizbike, I believe, will be just as attractive to women as it is to men. I like the idea of having it in one colour only, but I feel that the black packaging limits its appeal for women

- Because I believe this bicycle could be phenomenally popular, I suspect that the suggested price of £499 is too high

- A promotional event to coincide with the opening of Britain's byways would be an ideal opportunity to put the bike on the map – almost literally!

- I know just who we should get to advertise the Whizbike, and I'm pretty confident I could persuade him to do it. But we'll be after all the free publicity we can get, and I can see plenty of scope for that, too

To put together a detailed marketing document, with well-considered ideas, a range of options and a reasonably accurate budget (probably 12–15 pages in all), we would charge you £2,500. This, I can assure you, is far less than we would normally charge for the time involved, but then we really want this job!

Please let me know as soon as possible if this is OK with you, and we'll get working on the project more or less straight away. If you would like to contact me by phone, my direct line at the office is 0171 366 4329, or you can get hold of me over the weekend at 01344 765408. I look forward to hearing from you.

With best wishes and high hopes

Jane

Model e-mail 3

FROM: Sandra
TO: Mark
Subject: An idea

Do you know about Ann-Sophie Mütter, the luscious German violinist with the world at her feet? She is not only extremely beautiful, talented etc, but is a good interviewee and is travelling to just about every destination BA has ever touched down on, playing the complete cycle of Beethoven sonatas over the next year. She will be here in May and I could interview her. Possibly for *Travelling Life*. What think?

PS She is gorgeous enough for a cover.

***

FROM: Mark
TO: Sandra
Subject: An idea

Yup, would be on for that

Mark

***

FROM: Sandra
TO: Mark
Subject: Ann-Sophie Mütter

Excellent, I'll set it up. Any idea for which issue?

***

FROM: Mark
TO: Sandra
Subject: Ann-Sophie Mütter

Poss for August, but September more likely. Is she doing anything dramatic in those months?

***

FROM: Sandra
TO: Mark

As she is constantly travelling to perform the Beethoven sonata cycle we can say where you can see her and where she is going to be next. Her itinerary is phenomenal, there is virtually nowhere that remains unvisited. Her PR will sort out precisely where she'll be in September and let us know.

Sloppy grammar doesn't matter at all in this context. The important thing is to get the idea across. Expressive and economical language – 'luscious', 'gorgeous enough for a cover' – is chosen precisely because the writer is anticipating her editor's response – and she has anticipated well.

16. *Model Faxes and Memos*

Model fax 1

Fax

To:	Delia McBride	From:	William Chudleigh
Company:	Conferences Unlimited	Pages:	1 (including this cover sheet)
Fax:	0171 580 6241	Date:	3 March 1998

Re: Conference Venue

Hargrave House, four miles outside Northampton, looks perfect for our series of one-day seminars in September. It is a beautiful Georgian house in well-kept grounds, and is now used entirely as a conference centre. The main auditorium seats a maximum of 100, and there are two other rooms which can accommodate 20–30. The smaller of these is the morning room (max: 20 people), and this looks perfect for our purposes.

The morning room is pale yellow, with white ceiling and cornices, decorated with a mixture of modern watercolours and architectural prints. As you might expect, it gets the morning sun, which means you usually have to use the blinds. But during breaks in the proceedings, you can open the French windows, and everyone can step out on to the lawn to stretch their legs. The room has all the equipment we need – Powerpoint projector and computer (we simply have to provide the disk), white board, flip chart and OHP if needed. Also the chairs and tables can be moved around. There is plenty of space. Mineral water is provided in the room.

It only costs £150 to hire the room for the day. But if we hire it for the day, we must buy the rest of the package (which is obviously where Hargrave House makes money). Coffee and tea are £1.50 a head (delivered to the room at around 10.45am and 3.45pm, and lunch is £12.50 a head, for all you can eat (a choicse of two hot dishes, plus extensive cold buffet) and drink (mineral water, coke, fruit juices). There is a licensed bar, for which you pay. The restaurant is another very attractive room, and lunch breaks are staggered, so that we would break either 15 minutes before or 15 minutes after the occupants of the main auditorium.

There is a swimming pool, a tennis court and changing rooms (all relatively hidden at the back of the house), on which the hirers of the main auditorium get first option. If they don't take it up, Hargrave House will let us know at least two weeks in advance. If we are allowed to use the pool and tennis court, the manager will give us four free vouchers, but after that, there is a charge of £5 per head.

Excluding the swimming pool etc, Hargrave House would cost us £460 for the day (assuming the full 20 delegates). I hope you agree that this is exceptional value.

Model fax 2

To:	All delegates	From:	William Chudleigh
Company:	Conferences Unlimited	Pages:	1 (including this cover sheet)
Fax:	0171 580 6241	Date:	3 March 1998

Hargrave House: how to get there by road

Hargrave House is four miles outside Northampton. Whether you approach from North or South, you need to turn off the M1 at Junction 21. The A626 crosses the M1 at this point, so if you are coming from the West, the same applies.

From North, South or West:

1. At junction 21 on the M1, turn eastwards, following signs to **Northampton,** on the A626. Stay on this road for two miles, passing a Shell garage on your left.
2. About 400 yards after Shell garage, there is a crossroads. Turn left here, following signs to **Long Brendon** and **Flitchet.** Carry on for about a mile and a half, through Long Brendon, and up the hill, passing **The Crooked Billet** pub on your left.
3. Just 100 yards after The Crooked Billet, turn right, following the sign to **Hargrave**. Carry on for about half a mile. Look out for a tall stone wall on your left. The road curves to the left, and Hargrave House is signposted on your left. Enter through the main gates and follow signs to the car park.

From the East:

1. Take the A626 westwards, bypassing Northampton (if you are coming from Northampton, just head south until you hit the ring road). Keep on this road for about two miles, following signs for **Daventry**.
2. Look out for a large pub on your left, called the **Lear Arms**. At the crossroads 200 yards further on, turn right, following signs to **Long Brendon** and **Flitchet.** Carry on for about a mile and a half, through Long Brendon, and up the hill, passing **The Crooked Billet** pub on your left.
3. Just 100 yards after The Crooked Billet, turn right, following the sign to **Hargrave.** Carry on for about half a mile. Look out for a tall stone wall on your left. The road curves to the left, and Hargrave House is signposted on your left. Enter through the main gates and follow signs to the car park.

Model memo 1

To:	Everyone	**From:**	Rupert Morris
Re:	Christmas Party	**Date:**	4 November 1998

Bob and I went to *Carlo's*, the trendy new café/bar in Bolsover Street, yesterday. They have a private room for up to 50 people upstairs, which they showed us round. It costs nothing to book, provided you eat their food and drink their drink. Well, we tried the food and it was great – nice fresh salads, homemade pasta, salamis etc. House wine is only £7.99 a bottle, and they've got real ale and several good lagers on draught.

Here's our plan. We can bring in our own DJ and we reckon we could do the whole thing for £25 to £30 a head – less the £500 the company has kindly agreed to contribute. This should reduce the cost per head to around £10 to £15.

But of course, all this depends on final numbers. So if you're interested, please put your name here (+ the names of any partner or guests you would like to bring). We've provisionally booked December 12 from 8pm onwards. We've also sent this memo by letter, fax and e-mail to all the sales team and other members of staff working outside this office.

All enquiries to me on ext 209 (room 13 on the fifth floor).

Names here, please:

Model memo 2

To:	Celia Trumble, Managing Director
From:	Alan Tichbury, Head of Corporate Communications
Re:	Annual Report
Date:	3 April 1998

Now that the annual report is printed, to general if not unanimous approval, I hope you will allow me to suggest how we might tackle this job better next year. Above all, I am now convinced that we should hire an external writer.

From conception to printing, this project has taken me six months. During January and February it was an overwhelming concern, and there were several occasions when I was obliged to neglect other important jobs that would normally have taken priority. My colleague Tim Thompson has had to handle a number of tasks, particularly dealing with the press, which would normally be my reponsibility. While he has managed extremely well, and there have been no disasters, there have been points at which certain issues could and should have been handled differently.

The closure of the Bournemouth plant, for instance, was not managed as it might have been. If I hadn't been conducting inter-views in Basingstoke that week, I would certainly have contacted the *Evening Echo* and ensured that the right people were appropriately briefed. Even now, I am still catching up with issues I feel I should have addressed several weeks ago.

The annual report is a thankless task for any in-house writer – not least because everyone has different ideas about what it should say. Despite my best efforts, it has proved impossible to avoid arguments – sometimes quite bitter ones – between various departments. When I have to resolve these arguments, inevitably favouring one director or department over another, I am acutely aware of putting backs up – which makes it that much more difficult for me to do my normal job.

This is not special pleading, I assure you. I am thick-skinned enough to cope with occasional resentment, and next time I shall certainly try to eliminate some of these arguments by more careful advance consultation, but I still don't think that this is the best use of our staff resources. If the company is to present a unified face to the world, the last thing we want is for people to fall out with the corporate communications department.

If we were to hire an external writer, it need only involve minimal extra expense. More than half the cost could come out of my own budget, as we shall be able to make corresponding savings on our own staff pay and expenses. I can suggest several excellent writers. I would, of course, retain overall project control, and I believe this would enable me to maintain a clearer vision.

Please let me know what you think.

Index

Index

A Little More Help?

Rupert Morris is the founder and chief executive
of **Clarity** *(business solutions – in writing)*,
a consultancy which offers

- training programmes
- speeches
- reports
- ghost-writing
- seminars

For further details, contact **Clarity** at
6 Adam Street, London WC2N 6AA
Tel: 0171 379 8812 Fax: 0171 497 1441
e-mail: clarity@globalnet.co.uk

or call

07000 4 WORDS
(07000 496737)
or visit Clarity's website:
www.clarity4words.co.uk